In Pursuit of Their Dreams:

A History of Azorean Immigration
to the United States

Jerry R. Williams

In Pursuit of Their Dreams:

*A History of Azorean Immigration
to the United States*

2nd Edition

Center for Portuguese Studies and Culture
University of Massachusetts Dartmouth
North Dartmouth, Massachusetts
2007

PORTUGUESE IN THE AMERICAS SERIES
General Editor: Frank F. Sousa
Social Sciences Editor: Andrea Klimt
Editorial Manager: Gina M. Reis
Manuscript Editor and Copyeditor: Richard Larschan and Gina M. Reis
Graphic Designer: Spencer Ladd
Typesetter: Inês Sena
Photographic Consultant: Jay Avila

In Pursuit of Their Dreams: A History of Azorean Immigration to the United States
/ by Jerry Williams (2nd edition, University of Massachusetts, Dartmouth)
Copyright © 2005 by University of Massachusetts, Dartmouth, Reprint with
revisions 2007.

We gratefully acknowledge The Center for Migration Studies of New York, Inc.,
which published the first and second editions under the title of *And yet they
come: Portuguese Immigration from the Azores to the United States*. *In Pursuit of
Their Dreams: A History of Azorean Immigration to the United States* is an updated
and revised version of *And yet they come: Portuguese Immigration from the Azores to
the United States*. Library of Congress Catalog Number 82-71501, ISBN 0-
913256-57-9 (Cloth) 0-913256-60-9 (Paper), Copyright 1983.

The publication of *In Pursuit of Their Dreams: A History of Azorean
Immigration to the United States* was made possible in part by generous grants
from the Government of the Autonomous Region of the Azores and the
Luso-American Foundation.

Printed by RPI Printing, Fall River, MA

Library of Congress Cataloging-in-Publication Data
Williams, Jerry R. In pursuit of their dreams : a history of Azorean immigration to the
United States / Jerry R. Williams. -- 2nd ed. p. cm. -- (Portuguese in the Americas
series) Includes bibliographical references. ISBN 1-933227-19-2 (pbk. : alk. paper)
1. Azorean Americans--History. 2. Portuguese Americans--History. 3. Azoreans--
United States--History. 4. Azorean Americans--Social conditions. 5. Portuguese
Americans--Social conditions. 6. Azoreans--United States--Social conditions. 7.
Ethnic neighborhoods--United States--History. 8. Azores--Emigration and immigra-
tion--History. 9. United States--Emigration and immigration--History. I. University
of Massachusetts Dartmouth. Center for Portuguese Studies and Culture. II. Title.
E184.A95W55 2007
973'.0469104699--dc22   2007030033

TABLE OF CONTENTS

LIST OF MAPS

LIST OF FIGURES

To the grandchildren of John and Sally Avila.
May they all pursue their dreams.

Acknowledgements

I want to thank Frank Sousa of the Center for Portuguese Studies and Culture at the University of Massachusetts Dartmouth for his untiring efforts on behalf of this book and his enthusiastic support of the project from its conception. Larry Williams graciously did all of the cartographic work for the book. I am grateful to Muncel Chang for sharing his family history and photographs from Hawaii and to Joanne Stephens for contributing her family pictures from California. My long-time colleague and friend Bruce Bechtol provided continuing encouragement and support, usually over a cup of coffee. My wife Terry has always been an enthusiastic supporter of whatever project I am engrossed in and I do appreciate that. Most importantly, I want to acknowledge and thank Andrea Klimt for her editorial accomplishments; they are greatly appreciated. I also would like to pay tribute to all of the informants in this country and in the Azores who so graciously answered my questions and shared their personal stories. This is their story and I hope they find it worthwhile.

NEW DIRECTIONS AND FUTURE POSSIBILITIES:
UNDERSTANDING THE PORTUGUESE IMMIGRANT STORY[1]

ANDREA KLIMT

UNIVERSITY OF MASSACHUSETTS

DARTMOUTH

Jerry Williams' richly detailed history of Azorean immigration to the
United States offers us a solid foundation for understanding the experience and culture of Portuguese immigrants and their descendents.
Starting with the whaling routes that first connected the mid-Atlantic
archipelago with the ports of call in New England and California in the
early 1800s, Williams lays out the complex relationship between the
Azores and the United States that has continued into the present. We
learn how particular patterns of poverty, overpopulation, and social
inequality in the Azores pushed large numbers of the islands' inhabitants to leave their homes in search of better opportunities for themselves and their children. He tells the story of how the early whalers
who jumped ship in New Bedford, San Francisco, or Hawaii were followed by kin and fellow villagers who had heard of plentiful jobs in
New England's textile mills, gold and land in California, or agricultural
work in Hawaii. Williams' deft incorporation of first-hand narratives
and in-depth historical account allows us to gain insight into the
importance of family and community connections throughout the
immigrants' arduous transition from peasant village to industrial society.

One of the fascinating aspects of the Portuguese story is the striking
persistence of extremely concentrated coastal settlement patterns—
almost all Portuguese-American communities are found in either
California or along the Northeastern Seaboard. Williams explains how
the combination of regionally-specific economic opportunities and heavy
reliance on chain migration have, over the past century-and-a-half, led to
this particular distribution. His account gives a comprehensive overview
of how Portuguese-Americans—now numbering about a million people—have come to constitute a vibrant and highly visible presence within

southeastern New England, the areas around San Francisco and San Diego, Hawaii, and the New Jersey/New York metropolitan area.

An extremely important contribution of this work to our understanding of Portuguese-American immigration is Williams' attention to the differences between these various settlement regions. Even though all Azorean immigrants came from very similar backgrounds and with very similar aspirations, the economic and social conditions of the areas of the United States in which they settled were quite different from one another. Those regional differences have, Williams argues, variously shaped Portuguese-American communities into the present day. The typical New England experience, for example, of living in urban, predominantly Portuguese neighborhoods and working in factories with few options for social mobility contrasted sharply with the tendency amongst Azorean immigrants in California to buy land, become independent and sometimes very successful farmers, and live in dispersed rural communities. The trajectory was different in yet another way in Hawaii, where Azoreans were imported as plantation laborers and found themselves on the bottom of a very stratified social hierarchy with few attractive options open to them outside of leaving for the mainland or becoming less "Portuguese." Williams asks fascinating questions about how these significant differences in economic opportunity structures, settlement patterns, and place within local social arrangements have contributed to differences in patterns of social mobility, attitudes towards being "Portuguese," and degrees of cultural continuity. In contrast to many other studies of the Portuguese-American experience that focus primarily on single communities, Williams opens our eyes to key differences within that experience. His analysis sets up an extremely useful comparative framework that forces us to develop a more differentiated understanding of the various trajectories of Azoreans in the United States.

In Pursuit of Their Dreams pushes us, as many good books do, to ask new questions about what is still a relatively understudied immigrant group. The following sections outline central themes suggested in Williams' work that have been explored by other researchers. The aim is *not* to offer a comprehensive overview of this literature, but to identify promising directions for future research.[2] This body of research is very exciting in that analyses of the Portuguese case help fill a significant gap in our understanding of the immigrant experience in North

America. A survey of this literature also makes apparent that explorations of the Portuguese experience in North America offer insight into broader questions that are at the forefront of social scientific inquiry. Anthropologists, sociologists, political scientists, and social geographers investigating connections between racial, ethnic and national identities as well as between citizenship, state policy, and transnational connections find this corner of the Portuguese diaspora a particularly fertile research site. Other central theoretical questions that are illuminated by considerations of the Portuguese case include relationships between expressive culture, political power, and visibility; the dynamics of gender, work and family in immigrant contexts; the social needs of minority populations and their moves towards political empowerment; and the impact of global configurations and diasporic frameworks on local histories of community formation. This body of work suggests intriguing questions about the Portuguese experience in North America that still await exploration.

xv

Race, Ethnicity, and Nationality

Williams' account focuses on Azoreans, who constitute by far the majority of Portuguese immigrants to the United States and Canada. There are, however, significant numbers of Portuguese-speaking immigrants who have come to the United States from different regions of present-day Portugal, including the mainland and Madeira, as well as from countries whose histories intersected with Portugal's colonial past, such as Cape Verde and Brazil. A fertile area of research is how these differences in place of origin from within the Lusophone world—and the concomitant differences in race, ethnicity, and nationality—play out in the immigrant context.

One of the most provocative investigations of the complex nature of "Portuguese" identity is Marilyn Halter's ethnography of Cape Verdeans in southeastern Massachusetts (Halter). She lays out the fascinating historical twists and turns of how changing discourses about race in the United States and major shifts in Portugal's national boundaries played out in the immigrant context as people of Cape Verdean descent tried to establish identities that made sense to themselves and the people around them. Cape Verde was officially part of

Portugal until achieving independence from Portugal in 1975—so in terms of citizenship and national identity, initial generations of immigrants from these islands off the coast of Africa came as "Portuguese." Post-independence generations, however, were officially designated as "Cape Verdean." Given the extensive mixing of Portuguese and African populations, Cape Verdeans range from being phenotypically "black" to very "white." Immigrants coming to the United States encountered racial categories and hierarchies based on the "one-drop rule" and a categorical and absolute opposition between black and white, a system that contrasts sharply with the one operating in Cape Verde where class, island origin, and nationality figured into a very complex and often fluid set of racial categories not based on blood or phenotype. Halter documents Cape Verdean immigrant families in which the grandparents continue to declare themselves to be "white Portuguese"—regardless of their skin color—while their grandchildren declare themselves as "Cape Verdean," "African-American," and "black"—even though the distinction between being African-American and Cape Verdean has no resonance within the wider American context. Halter's exploration of the complex argument about what it means to be "black" or "white" in relation to what it means to be "Portuguese" or "Cape Verdean" or "African-American" highlights what happens when very different ideas about race are brought together through the process of immigration. Questions about how subsequent generations of Cape-Verdean Americans negotiate racial, ethnic, and national identities remain open.

Another key question that is as yet unanswered is how immigrants from different points in the wider Lusophone world relate to one another. In recent years, for example, the Brazilian immigrant population has grown dramatically in areas with well-established Portuguese-American communities in the northeastern United States and researchers are beginning to investigate the complicated relationship between these two groups. Brazilians and Azoreans may share a language, historical intersections, and social and educational needs, but they have very different cultural values and styles and at times pursue divergent political agendas.

Differences in regional origin within Portugal itself also play out in the immigrant context in ways that are not well documented. Williams focuses almost exclusively on the story of the Azorean immigrant experience, but explorations of the relationship between people from different islands of the Azores as well as between Azoreans and other Portuguese from the continent and Madeira would tell us a great deal about how individuals negotiate identities and create communities in the immigrant context. When do people resort to local or regional identities such as *Micalense* or Azorean? When is an all-encompassing "Portuguese" identity asserted across regional differences? And what are the lines of argument between compatriots on how to "be Portuguese"?

The patterns of chain migration, so well documented by Williams, have led to communities in the United States that are linked to particular regions, islands, even villages in Portugal. The community in Newark, New Jersey, for example, is primarily comprised of recent immigrants from the continent; the more-established communities of southeastern Massachusetts are primarily from the Azores, principally São Miguel; and areas of the Central Valley in California are linked to other Azorean islands such as Terceira. It would be fascinating to further develop Williams' comparative perspective with explorations of how these differences in place of origin intersect with regionally specific histories in shaping the cultural, social, and political landscapes of different Portuguese-American communities.

Citizenship, the State, and Transnational Connections

Work on the Portuguese case has made significant contributions to our understanding of how immigrants think about citizenship and national belonging and negotiate connections with their communities of origin. Social scientists working in this area have demonstrated how the policies of multiple states shape the options and sentiments of transnational migrants and point to the necessity of situating individuals' lives within overarching, often global, political dynamics.

State policies of the sending society clearly shape migrant trajectories and identities. Brettell offers insight into how contradictions between Portugal's official emigration policy and the actual practices of border regulation determined where and under what circumstances its citizens could go (Brettell 2005a). In an attempt to control the massive hemorrhaging of its population, the Portuguese government in the 19th and then the 20th century under Salazar restricted the issuing of passports and required potential emigrants to provide proof of military service. The state, however, simultaneously encouraged illegal emigration through the purposely lax enforcement of border controls. Many men were thus forced into leaving wives and children behind. The endemic and massive emigration of people who were still tied to their homeland ensured a continued flow of remittances back to Portugal, promoted the establishment of profitable trade markets in various corners of the diaspora and, perhaps most importantly, diffused political dissatisfaction with an oppressive *status quo* at home. Through its contradictory stances, Brettell argues that the Portuguese state encouraged its citizens to leave, remain connected to Portugal, but not come home.

Feldman-Bianco has explored the impact of more recent developments in the policies of the Portuguese state on the identities and options of Portuguese migrants (Feldman-Bianco 1994). She chronicles Portugal's efforts to incorporate its diaspora into the body of the nation and to legally and symbolically uncouple national membership from the geography of residence. Portuguese migrants have the option of dual citizenship open to them and are actively encouraged by the Portuguese state to maintain connections with their country of origin and to promote Portuguese language and culture within their ethnic communities. *Saudade* is thus both a heart-felt sentiment and a state-supported policy. These new patterns of transnational connection and emergence of multi-centered arenas of belonging are key areas for future research.

Other social scientists have focused on the impact of state policies of receiving societies on the identities and options of Portuguese immigrants in North America. Bloemraad explores the question of why the Portuguese immigrants in Canada acquire citizenship in their new home at a significantly higher and faster rate than the Portuguese who have settled in the United States (Bloemraad 2002a). The two populations have comparable histories and backgrounds, and both countries are liberal democracies with established and legally similar ways of acquiring citizenship. Her comparison reveals that the ways in which the naturalization process is handled in the two countries accounts for the different naturalization rates she observed: in Canada, immigrants are actively encouraged and supported in their efforts to acquire Canadian citizenship; in the United States immigrants have to negotiate a rather unwelcoming bureaucracy on their own and receive little or no government support during the process of acquiring American citizenship.

Also working in Canada on the impact of state policies on immigration and naturalization, Giles demonstrates how Canada's immigrant selection system gives preference to men with established professions and disadvantages women who often enter the country as dependents without education or professional training (Giles). Differential treatment at the point of entry into the country, Giles argues, contributes to divergences between the trajectories of men and women as they attempt to achieve economic success and social mobility in their new home.

A more specific case of the consequences of state policy is explored by Moniz as he documents the experiences of Portuguese resident aliens who have been deported from the United States for felony violations (Moniz). American, except for their passports, these people are sent to homelands they have never known, forced to leave family and friends behind, and live in a place where they do not know the language and have no ready sources of social or financial support. Moniz shows the dire consequences of a definition of national belonging that allows no discretionary room in its implementation.

One of the interesting directions for future work on citizenship and forms of local and multi-local forms of belonging is to compare the situations of people in various corners of the Portuguese diaspora with the trajectories commonly found in the United States and Canada. As Williams points out so well in his work, comparison often helps us examine taken-for-granted assumptions and, in this case, develop more differentiated understandings of how people forge connections and identities. Brettell's comparative analysis of community formation and degrees of connection with Portugal among the Portuguese migrants in Toronto and Paris illustrates the usefulness of this approach (Brettell 2005b). The geographically cohesive and institutionally complete communities and patterns of permanent settlement characteristic of many immigrant communities in North America that many social scientists have come to consider as inevitable are not present in Paris. At the time of Brettell's research in the 1970s, the Portuguese were scattered throughout the city, had no cohesive community replete with ethnic institutions, and maintained active transnational connections to natal villages.

Klimt's work on the Portuguese who emigrated to Germany makes a similar point about how trajectories of belonging amongst transnational migrants, attitudes towards citizenship, and relationships with their homeland are very much shaped by the social and political dynamics in the receiving society (Klimt 2000). Despite their now over three decades of residence in Germany, most Portuguese have no interest in acquiring German citizenship and, in contrast to their compatriots in North America with similar histories, reject the notion of exclusively locating their futures within their new countries of residence. Klimt also draws a comparison between the trajectories of Portuguese immigrants in Germany and those in France (Klimt 2004). The contrast between rates of naturalization, nature of connection to communities of origin, and patterns of ethnic and national identity formation draws attention to the impact of state policy on the development of immigrant identities.

Following a similar comparative approach, Noivo pursues the interesting question of how Portuguese immigrants in Australia and Canada forge very different kinds of connections with their homeland and with compatriots across the diaspora. She also points to the impact of the Portuguese state's efforts to keep its far-flung emigrants "Portuguese" (Noivo 2002). Given the long and varied history of Portuguese emigration to almost every continent, the possibilities for comparative research within this diaspora are particularly promising.

Expressive Culture, Self-representation, and Identity

In Williams' account, we learn of the importance of rituals and traditions for the newly-arrived immigrants from the Azores. Recent work on expressive culture of migrants in various corners of the Lusophone world has further explored forms of ethnic self-representation and their complex connections to the politics of identity formation. The question of how and why people publicly assert their "Portugueseness"—or, as is often the case with post-colonial populations, of their *not* being Portuguese—offers insight into local negotiations for political power, social status, and economic gain.

Cases from the recent diaspora illustrate the important role public displays of culture play in arguments about identity and political power. Holton investigated how folkloric performances figure prominently into the consolidation of a positive ethnic identity and audible political voice amongst the Portuguese in Newark, New Jersey (Holton 2004, 2005). Participation in folklore troupes helps keep the second generation within the networks and traditional values of the Portuguese-American community and folkloric performances give the Portuguese prominence within state politics that celebrate and promote multiculturalism. The film, *The Flight of the Dove,* directed by Nancy da Silveira, makes similiar points as it shows how the Holy Ghost Feasts in Californian communities help keep people of Portuguese descent connected to one another and to a sense of "being Portuguese."

By going a bit further afield, Klimt argues that the visibility of expressive culture does not always correspond to increased access to political power (Klimt 2005). In the case she investigates in Germany, Portuguese folkloric performances gained a very high level of visibility on the local scene, but in a context where most Portuguese are not citizens and have no voting rights, that cultural prominence did not translate into political voice or pressure to change the *status quo.*

Sieber's work on musical production within the Cape Verdean diaspora brings the complex dynamics of post-colonial relations and increasingly fluid global interconnections into our understandings of immigrant identity formation (Sieber). The Cape Verdean musicians he works with who live in and around the Boston area assertively reject any histories of connection with Portugal and produce musical forms that incorporate both traditional forms from the islands as well as contemporary innovations encountered in the diaspora. His case challenges the widespread assumption that the cultural self-representation of immigrant populations always emphasizes tradition and an unbroken continuity with the past and the homeland.

Examples from the temporally more distant diaspora further illuminate the complex relationship between expressive culture and historically particular relations of power and help us place the more familiar cases from the United States and Canada into a boarder context. Sarkissian relates the fascinating story of the town of Malacca, a one-time Portuguese colonial outpost in Malaysia dating back to the 15th century (Sarkissian 2000, 2002). There, a community composed of people who are five centuries removed from any direct contact with Portugal and whose "blood" connections are tenable at best, actively promotes itself as "Portuguese." She shows how being "Portuguese" and performing "Portuguese culture"—much of which was locally invented and authenticated—has provided economic and political advantages in the postcolonial making of Malaysia.

Taking us to another temporally distant diasporic outpost in Santa Catarina, Brazil, where the original arrival of immigrants from the Azores goes back over five generations, Leal documents the revival of a cultural identity that had already been largely lost (Leal 2002, 2005). In contrast to the Malaysian case, this process of identity formation draws on a discourse of continuity and authenticity in efforts to assert that local culture is in fact "Azorean." In the Brazilian case, "being Azorean" has become important within local struggles over political power and this claim is validated by renewed connections with the ancestral homeland.

There are still many fascinating questions about the connection between expressive culture, immigrant identity, and political power that await the attention of future researchers. Further work on the form and meaning of cultural performance and its relationship to trajectories of identity formation, patterns of social relations, and access to political power would shed light on the question of what happens to ethnic identity and culture over the generations (Almeida). Will ethnicity over third, fourth, fifth generations be expressed through primarily symbolic means? Will groups with different relations to political power develop different forms of expressive culture? What aspects of culture will be retained, changed, or cast off? The dramatic contrasts between the different corners of the Portuguese diaspora invite further reflection on how historical context shapes these questions about the cultural identities of immigrants and their descendents.

Gender, Family, and Work

Williams' account of immigrants' work experiences—whether in New England's textile mills and garment factories, the gold fields and dairy farms of California, or 19th century whalers and 20th century fishing vessels—sets the wider context for investigations of the intertwined dynamics of change in the arenas of gender, family, and work. First-generation immigrants not only had to learn new ways of earning a living, but had to confront challenges that these new work arrangements as well as the new culture around them posed to their ideas about the roles of men and women and family. In immigrant contexts where both men and women worked outside the house and earned incomes, questions arose as to who took care of home and children and made decisions and had authority within the family. In immigrant households, it is often the second-generation children who must navigate between the expectations of their parents and the possibilities presented by the wider American society. Deeply-held values about the relations between parents and children or the obligations and options of sons versus daughters—who can go out without a chaperone; who is responsible for household chores; who can leave the household before marriage; who can hold what kinds of jobs; who controls the earnings of family members; etc.—often frame the discussions in immigrant households.

Such tensions within first-generation families around cultural change have drawn the attention of a number of anthropologists. In her ethnography of Portuguese families in Canada, Noivo investigates how expectations of family cohesiveness, mutual assistance, and gender-specific roles lead to familial conflict as the second and third generations, especially the daughters, explore options of independence and individual social mobility (Noivo 1997). She offers insight into how inequalities within the family along the lines of gender and generation exacerbate the strains incurred by transnational migration, working-class status, and minority group membership.

Also working in Canada, Giles traces the transition from first-generation Portuguese immigrant women—who tend to work in manufacturing or domestic service, left school at the elementary level, and have limited skills in English and few realistic options for further education—to their second-generation daughters, who tend to work in low-level, white-collar jobs and, despite discrimination in the schools and often ambivalent family attitudes towards education, have often finished high school and in some cases attended college (Giles). Giles pays special attention to the dilemmas of second-generation women who attempt to navigate beyond constraining gender roles while maintaining their commitment to family and community.

A more historical perspective on these questions is offered by Lamphere in her examination of the transformations in the roles of immigrant mothers and their daughters since the early 20th century in a New England urban center (Lamphere). She explores the creative ways in which different generations of Portuguese (and Columbian) women cope with the demands industrial work places on themselves and their families. Judging from the impassioned debates among my students about the tensions between familial and community expectations and the aspirations of second and third-generation children, there are still many issues awaiting exploration.

A stereotype often associated with the Portuguese is that of the docile worker who was socialized to not question the *status quo* or challenge oppressive labor practices. The results of a number of studies challenge this assumption. In a study of unionization in a Boston electronics factory, Bookman queries the validity of this image (Bookman). She finds that Portuguese immigrant women in this case not only joined the union and took on self-empowering roles, but mobilized kin and community-based experiences and networks in building workplace solidarity. The major role of Portuguese immigrants in the unionization of New England's textile industry is documented by Reeve in his life histories of union organizers and history of union activity in southeastern Massachusetts (Reeve). And in Feldman-Bianco's wonderful film, *Saudade*, we hear an elderly woman's rendition of "On a Picket Line" as she reminisces about her participation in the famous New England textile strike of 1928. Clearly, coming of age under Salazar, being a recent immigrant, or the fact of being female did not prevent Portuguese immigrants from contributing to labor activism. It is also clear that there are many more stories to be told about the attitudes and actions of past and present-day Portuguese-American and Portuguese immigrant workers.

Education, Social Needs, and Political Participation

The social and educational needs of an immigrant and largely working-class ethnic population are obviously topics of relevance and concern. They are also topics that have, at least with regards to the Lusophone populations of the United States and Canada, been largely understudied. In a recent review of research on the academic achievement of Portuguese-Canadian youth, Nunes concludes that the available evidence "is often fragmented, unsubstantiated by research, child-centered, culturally biased and contradictory... [and that] [f]ew works have sought to investigate in depth the complex linkages between scholastic underachievement and the Luso-Canadian community's marginalized role within Canada" (Nunes 1). Although there has been some attention in Canada to heritage-language education (Helms-Park) as well as to the dilemmas faced by the second generation as they negotiate their identities and aspirations for education and social mobility within culturally complex worlds (Oliveira and Teixeira), there still remains much work to be done on the educational and social needs of this population.

This is also the case on the southern side of the border. In an article based on ethnographic research in an urban high school in southeastern Massachusetts, Becker raised important questions about the challenges faced by the children of newly-arrived Portuguese immigrants as they enter American schools (Becker). She points to how low expectations and negative stereotypes held by teachers contributed to an atmosphere that made it difficult for first-generation immigrant children to assert a positive connection with their cultures and identities in the school context and mitigated their ability to imagine and realize academic success. There has been research documenting the systematic academic underachievement of Portuguese-American children, work on bilingualism and heritage-language instruction, and reflections on the social service needs of this population (Mulcahy), but this is clearly an area in need of innovative and systematic investigation.

The question of why the Portuguese do not have a higher profile in regional or national politics has perplexed observers for quite some time. In a very provocative article on the role of ethnic brokers in the Portuguese community of Toronto, Brettell described how the professionals and leaders of the community contributed—through their positions as brokers and patrons—to the insulation of their ethnic constituents from the surrounding society (Brettell 2005c). These important questions about the emergence of ethnic leaders, their role in influencing an ethnic community's collective access to political power, and the extent of participation by Portuguese-Americans in the political process have been taken up in several recent studies. A collected volume on the political perspectives of Portuguese-Americans in

Massachusetts examines attitudes to such key issues as education and foreign language instruction, the economy and access to jobs and social mobility, and a range of other social issues such as immigration policy, abortion, and school prayer (Barrow). This collection also explored the patterns of relatively low degrees of participation in the political process and why, in a region with such a large and concentrated Portuguese-American population, not more of the political leaders stem from this community. An in-depth comparative study by Bloemraad of the political incorporation of Portuguese immigrants in the United States and Canada sheds further light on how government policy impacts the development of community leaders and advocates (Bloemraad 2002b).

There are many assumptions about why Portuguese-Americans are not as politically vocal as many other ethnic groups, foremost of which is the argument that coming of age under fascism, where political action was systematically suppressed, led to immigrants with little interest or experience in politics. But the validity of that argument is clearly receding with the passage of time—and some argue that it never adequately accounted for patterns of political inactivity in the immigrant context. These recent studies point to important questions that merit investigation.

Local Voices and Histories of Community Formation

Williams pushes us to think carefully about both the commonalities framing the Portuguese-American experience *and* the significant differences characterizing communities in the various regions of settlement. There are a number of studies in the United States as well as Canada that further contribute to our understanding of the various ways in which Portuguese populations organize their communities.

Portuguese emigration to Canada is fairly recent with the first arrival of immigrants from the Azores dating back only to the early 1950s. The histories of the ethnic communities in Montreal, Toronto, and Quebec brought together in the book, *The Portuguese in Canada* (Teixeira and Da Rosa), show us how tight family and village connections, state policies that fostered chain migration, and the nature of local housing markets helped create urban communities that were geographically concentrated, institutionally complete and vibrant, and culturally fairly homogeneous (Lavigne and Teixeira, Da Rosa and Teixeira, Teixeira). These studies trace changing settlement patterns over time and reflect on the patterned connections to social mobility, language retention, and cultural assimilation.

The similarities with many Portuguese-American communities is striking, but it would be a very productive next step to systematically explore the comparison between American communities that include fourth and fifth-generation ethnics and those in Canada that consist primarily of first-generation immigrants and their now adult children. Holton's work in New Jersey, where the immigrant community is relatively recent and concerns with maintaining connections with the homeland and the authenticity of ethnic culture are more intense than in the older New England communities, further suggests the usefulness of contextualizing specific cases within a larger comparative framework (Holton 2004).

xxvii

The transformation of an ethnic community over time and the relevance of local politics and economic structures is taken up by several studies in New England. An older study by Beck offers us an account of a neighborhood in Providence, Rhode Island where successive generations of newly-arrived Azorean and Cape Verdean immigrants had settled since the late 19th century (Beck). Although they lived side-by-side in the same area of the city and were both officially "Portuguese," Cape Verdeans were subject to the racial hierarchies of the United States in ways that their Azorean counterparts were not. Beck tells the story of the complex relationship between these connected, but still quite separate immigrant groups, who were both subjected to the geographic and social upheaval brought about by massive urban renewal. The question raised by this study—and by Halter's work mentioned earlier—concerns the local variability of the relationships between Azorean and Cape Verdean communities. It is an intertwined history, but we may ask whether the trajectories of individual and community relations always look the same in different contexts. In rural areas of Cape Cod, for example, the economic interdependencies and close social interrelationships are quite different from the social geographies of Boston, where Azorean communities are geographically quite distant from Cape Verdean neighborhoods and patterns of social connection seem to be framed by race-based antagonisms and affinities. Sieber has documented the significance of connections between Cape Verdeans in

Boston and other immigrant groups of color, which sound significantly different from the relationships between ethnic groups in less urban areas of southeastern Massachusetts (Sieber).

Hearing the voices of the immigrants themselves is essential to understanding the immigrant experience. Two related projects from southeastern Massachusetts very effectively establish the value of hearing about individual lives. The edited volume, *Portuguese Spinner,* brings together a wealth of stories based on oral histories of individual migrants and gives us real insight into what it is like to leave one's homeland behind and make a fresh start in a new and strange place (Thomas and McCabe). The film *Saudade,* by Feldman-Bianco, also vividly documents the life stories of Portuguese immigrants to this region and makes clear that there is no substitute for literally hearing people's individual accounts. There are a number of projects across the country that will make extensive collections of oral histories and archival materials documenting the Portuguese-American experience available to future generations of researchers, and hopefully the present as well as the past voices of immigrants will continue to contribute to our understanding of the trajectories of Portuguese-Americans[3]

Global Configurations and Diasporic Frameworks

One of the reasons that the Portuguese-American story is so valuable to our efforts to understand the processes and experiences of transnational migration is that it is part of the much larger story of the Portuguese diaspora. As Brettell, Feldman-Bianco and others have pointed out, massive emigration has long been integral to the fabric of Portuguese society and the emigrant constitutes a national symbol that frames the lives and outlooks of almost every Portuguese citizen (Brettell 2005a, Feldman-Bianco 1992; see also Noivo 2000 and Rocha-Trindade). The Portuguese nation, in fact, has been increasingly defined as a deterritorialized entity that encompasses the far-flung diaspora as well as the erstwhile colonies that Portugal once dominated. The patterns of emigration—where people go, why they leave, as well as how they do or do not maintain connections with their homeland—have changed over the decades, as have the conditions at home that have long prompted people to leave (Baganha). An interesting twist to the long history of

Due to inclusion in the European Union. cf. Bill Ong Hing: Ethical Borders; chapter 4.

endemic emigration is that <u>Portugal has recently become a country</u> <u>which receives more immigrants than it sends forth.</u>

The challenging and revealing question is how the story of the Portuguese in North America fits into this larger story—that is, how do the historically particular conditions of this receiving society compare with those of other places that have received immigrants from Portugal (Klimt and Lubkemann). How do the politics and power relations, economies and opportunity structures, and status hierarchies characteristic of any particular society variously shape the identities and trajectories of its immigrants? Just as Williams explores how the Portuguese communities in New England, California, Hawaii, and New Jersey are shaped by regionally-specific conditions, we can ask how the paths of the Portuguese in the United States and Canada compare to those of their compatriots in Brazil, Germany, Malaysia, or any number of other countries around the world. The answers will deepen our understanding of the story of the Portuguese in North America.

References Cited

Almeida, Onésimo Teotónio. 2000. Value Conflicts and Cultural Adjustment in North America. In *The Portuguese in Canada,* ed. Carlos Teixeira and Victor Da Rosa, 112-24. Toronto: University of Toronto Press.

Baganha, Maria. 1999. Migrações internacionais de e para Portugal: o que sabemos e para donde vamos? *Revista crítica de ciências sociais* 52: 229-80.

Barrow, Clyde W., ed. 2002. *Portuguese-Americans and Contemporary Civic Culture in Massachusetts.* Dartmouth, MA: University of Massachusetts Dartmouth.

Beck, Sam. 1992. *Manny Almeida's Ringside Lounge: The Cape Verdeans' Struggle for their Neighborhood.* Providence: Gavea-Brown.

Becker, Adeline. 1990. The Role of the School in the Maintenance and Change of Ethnic Group Affiliation. *Human Organization* 49 (1): 48-55.

Bloemraad, Irene. 2002a. The North American Naturalization Gap: An Institutional Approach to Citizenship Acquisition in the United States and Canada. *International Migration Review* 36 (1): 193-228.

———. 2002b. Ethnic leaders and the Immigrant Settlement Industry: The Development of Community Advocates. Paper presented at the annual meeting of the American Sociological Association, August 2002, in Chicago, IL.

Bookman, Ann. 1988. Unionization in an Electronics Factory: The Interplay of Gender, Ethnicity, and Class. In *Women and the Politics of Empowerment,* ed. Ann Bookman and Sandra Morgan, 159-79. Philadelphia: Temple University Press.

Brettell, Caroline. [1993] 2003a. The Emigrant, the Nation, and the State in Nineteenth- and Twentieth-Century Portugal: An Anthropological Approach. In

Anthropology and Migration: Essays on Transnationalism, Ethnicity, and Identity, ed. Caroline Brettell, 9-22. Walnut Creek, CA: AltaMira Press.

[1981] 2003b. Is the Ethnic Community Inevitable?: A Comparison of the Settlement Patterns of Portuguese Immigrants in Toronto and Paris. In *Anthropology and Migration: Essays on Transnationalism, Ethnicity, and Identity*, ed. Caroline Brettell, 109-26. Walnut Creek, CA: AltaMira Press.

[1977] 2003c. Ethnicity and Entrepreneurs: Portuguese Immigrants in a Canadian City. In *Anthropology and Migration: Essays on Transnationalism, Ethnicity, and Identity*, ed. Caroline Brettell, 127-38. Walnut Creek, CA: AltaMira Press.

Da Rosa, Victor and Carlos Teixeira. 2000. The Portuguese Community in Quebec. In *The Portuguese in Canada*, ed. Carlos Teixeira and Victor Da Rosa, 191-206. Toronto: University of Toronto Press.

Feldman-Bianco, Bela. 1992. Multiple Layers of Time and Space: The Construction of Class, Race, Ethnicity, and Nationalism among Portuguese immigrants. In *Towards a Transnational Perspective on Migration: Race, Class, Ethnicity, and Nationalism Reconsidered*, ed. N.G. Schiller, L. Basch, and C. Blanc-Szanton, 145-74. New York: New York Academy of Sciences.

1994. Immigration, Saudade, and the Dialectics of Deterritorialization and Reterritorialization. Paper presented at Wenner Gren Foundation for Anthropological Research, Symposium no. 117, *Transnationalism, Nation-State Building, and Culture*, 1994, in Mijas, Spain.

Giles, Wenona. 2002. *Portuguese Women in Toronto: Gender, Immigration, and Nationalism*. Toronto: University of Toronto Press.

Halter, Marilyn. 1993. *Between Race and Ethnicity: Cape Verdean American Immigrants, 1860-1965*. Urbana: University of Illinois Press.

Helms-Park, Rena. 2000. Two Decades of Heritage Language Education. In *The Portuguese in Canada*, ed. Carlos Teixeira and Victor Da Rosa, 127-44. Toronto: University of Toronto Press.

Holton, Kimberly DaCosta. 2004. Dancing Along the In-Between: Folklore Performance and Transmigration in Portuguese Newark. *Portuguese Studies Review* 11 (2): 153-182.

2005. Pride, Prejudice, and Politics: Performing Portuguese Folklore Amid Newark's Urban Renaissance. *Etnográfica* IX (1): 81-102.

Klimt, Andrea. 2000. European Spaces: Portuguese Migrants' Notions of Home and Belonging. *Diaspora: A Journal of Transnational Studies* 9 (2): 259-85.

2004. Trajectórias Divergentes: os portugueses em França e na Alemanha. *Ler Historia* 46: 85-107.

2005. Performing Portugueseness in Germany. *Etnográfica* IX (1):103-22.

Klimt, Andrea, and Stephen Lubkemann. 2002. Argument across the Portuguese-speaking World: A Discursive Approach to Diaspora. *Diaspora: A Journal of Transnational Studies* 11 (2): 145-162.

Lamphere, Louise. 1987. *From Working Daughters to Working Mothers: Immigrant Women in a New England Industrial Community*. Ithaca: Cornell University Press.

Lavigne, Gilles, and Carlos Teixeira. 2000. Building a Neighborhood in Montreal. In *The Portuguese in Canada*, ed., Carlos Teixeira and Victor Da Rosa, 175-90. Toronto: University of Toronto Press.

Leal, João. 2002. Identities and Imagined Homelands: Reinventing the Azores in Southern Brazil. *Diaspora: A Journal of Transnational Studies* 11 (2): 233-54.

2005. We Are Azorean: Discourses and Practices of Folk Culture in Santa Catarina (Southern Brazil). *Etnográfica* IX (1): 171-194.

Moniz, Miguel. 2004. Exiled Home: Criminal Deportee Forced Return Migrants and Transnational Identity, the Azorean example. Ph.D. dissertation, Brown University.

Mulcahy, Maria da Gloria. 1998. The Immigrants Assistance Center. In *Portuguese Spinner: An American Story*, ed. Marsha L. McCabe and Joseph D. Thomas, 104-09. New Bedford, MA: Spinner Publications Inc.

Noivo, Edite. 1997. *Inside Ethnic Families: Three Generations of Portuguese–Canadians.* Montreal: McGill-Queen's University Press.

2000. Diasporic Indentities at Century's End. In *The Portuguese in Canada,* ed. Carlos Teixeira and Victor Da Rosa, 158-74. Toronto: University of Toronto Press.

2002. Towards a Cartography of Portugueseness: Challenging the Hegemonic Center. *Diaspora: A Journal of Transnational Studies* 11 (2): 158-74.

Nunes, Fernando. 2004. Portuguese-Canadian Youth and their Academic Underachievement: A Literature Review. *Portuguese Studies Review* 11 (2): 41-88.

Oliveira, Manuel Armando, and Carlos Teixeira. 2004. 'Second Generation,' Cultural Retention and Ethnic Identity: Young Portuguese and Portuguese-descendents in Canada. *Portuguese Studies Review* 11 (2): 1-23.

Reeve, Penn. 1998. The Portuguese Worker. In *Portuguese Spinner: An American Story*, ed., Marsha L. McCabe and Joseph D. Thomas, 230-35 New Bedford, MA: Spinner Publications Inc.

Rocha Trindade, Beatriz. 2000. The Portuguese Diaspora. In *The Portuguese in Canada*, ed., Carlos Teixeira and Victor Da Rosa, 15-33. Toronto: University of Toronto Press.

Sarkissian, Margaret. 2000. *D'Albuquerque's Children: Performing Tradition in Malaysia's Portuguese Settlement.* Chicago: The University of Chicago Press.

2002. Playing Portuguese: Constructing Identity in Malaysia's Portuguese Community. *Diaspora: A Journal of Transnational Studies* 11 (2): 215-232.

Sieber, Timothy. 2005. Popular Music and Cultural Identity in the Cape Verdean Post-Colonial Diaspora. *Etnográfica* IX: (1):123-48.

Teixeira, Carlos. 2000. On the Move: Portuguese in Toronto. In *The Portuguese in Canada*, ed. Carlos Teixeira and Victor Da Rosa, 207-22. Toronto: University of Toronto Press.

Teixeira, Carlos, and Victor Da Rosa, ed. 2000. *The Portuguese in Canada.* Toronto: University of Toronto Press.

Thomas, Joseph D., and Marsha L. McCabe, ed. 1998. *Portuguese Spinner: An American Story.* New Bedford, MA: Spinner Publications, Inc.

Notes

[1] I would like to thank the innumerable students who have participated in my "Portuguese in the Americas" class for teaching me about their lives and the Portuguese and Cape Verdean communities of southeastern Massachusetts. It is in conversations with them that many of the ideas in this essay were initially formulated. I would also like to thank the friends and colleagues–many of whom are cited in the bibliography–for their collaborative engagement with the themes of Portuguese emigration, culture, and identity formation. In particular I would like to express my appreciation to Caroline Brettell, Bela Feldman-Bianco, Mark Handler, Kimberly DaCosta Holton, João Leal, Stephen Lubkemann, Margaret Sarkissian, and Timothy Sieber. The gaps and shortcomings of the essay are obviously of my own making.

[2] There are numerous articles and academic theses on the Portuguese experience in North America that are, for reasons of space, not addressed in this essay. There is also a significant body of research on Portuguese migration in French that is extremely useful, but not included in this bibliography.

[3] Kimberly DaCosta Holton at Rutgers University has established a Portuguese Oral History Project that serves as a repository of her students' research on the New Jersey Portuguese community. At the University of Massachusetts, Dartmouth, Frank Sousa, Director of the Center for Portuguese Studies and Culture, is organizing a comprehensive Portuguese-American Archives that will be a central collection point of documents pertaining to the Portuguese in the United States.

1

This is a story of migration. It is about people who dreamed of a better life for themselves and their children and actively pursued those dreams by leaving the country of their birth to seek new opportunities in a foreign country. From nine small islands in the Atlantic Ocean, the Azores, came a group of immigrants who have made significant, but still little-recognized, contributions to American society (see Map 1). Their story is unique, in the sense that the experience of every one of the millions of immigrants who came to America is unique. Certainly for 19th century Azoreans, migration brought an abrupt end to a way of life that had changed little in the past century. The stability imparted from living in the same village where one's parents and their parents before them had lived was left behind in the search for an unknown replacement. They left behind their families and friends, a familiar way of life, a sense of belonging, and set out for a strange new land where the language was foreign and the customs unfamiliar. Although people of many diverse ethnic groups shared these experiences, for the individuals involved it was a very personal experience, the memories of which remained with them for the rest of their lives.[1]

Dreams rarely come true by themselves. Achieving a dream often involves a willingness to take a chance and actively pursue a goal that sometimes is nothing more than an idea or vague image in an individual's mind. To pursue a goal, however, one needs to believe that there is at least a chance for success. In the traditional Azorean society of the 19th and 20th centuries there was little prospect for change. Realistically, the choices for most people amounted to accepting their lives as they were and giving up on their dreams or leaving their homeland. Many

MAP I

AZORES

decided to take a chance and leave. Giving up a traditional existence in a familiar setting and becoming an emigrant in search of that dream was, in itself, no guarantee of success. Not everyone who departed the islands seeking a new life in America was successful. The challenges of learning a new language, finding a new occupation and conducting life in a new and totally foreign social setting were intense. Some soon realized that they preferred the stability of a traditional lifestyle to the unknown and constantly changing world characteristic of American society. In the face of hardships and sometimes just plain bad luck, some immigrants gave up on the American Dream and returned to their homeland.

Many of those who stayed on in America endured the difficulties and took advantage of opportunities they encountered. The occasional account of the brother, sister, uncle, cousin or acquaintance who was not only surviving in this huge new country, but had "made it big" continued to reinforce the dream that life could be better in America. These success stories of immigrants, frequently embellished and always transmitted by letter or word of mouth, continued to inspire Azoreans to join family members and friends already in America. People who heard these stories often reassessed their own situation and decided that they too wanted to realize their dreams. The tide of emigrants from the Azores ebbed and flowed for almost two hundred years in response to changing events in both the islands and the United States. Recurring hardships in the islands frequently served to push the inhabitants out of their traditional setting while opportunities in America acted like a giant magnet, pulling them out across the Atlantic Ocean to a new future.

The reception that Portuguese immigrants received in their new homeland varied by the areas in which they settled and the historically specific conditions. Being an immigrant and speaking broken English with a foreign accent was no great cause for concern in 19th century America. Economically and socially the country was expanding westward and immigrants provided much of the physical labor for that expansion. During the economic depression that followed World War I, the emergence of ideas like unionism, socialism and even communism were frequently associated with foreigners. Subsequent restrictions on new immigration, xenophobia, and even deportations of "undesirables" became more common and wide-spread. Optimistic after the defeat of fascism, post-World War II America opened its arms

3

to war refugees and foreign accents again became more common and non-threatening. In the last third of the 20th century, the worldwide triumph of democracy, capitalism and everything associated with being American has instilled a new self-confidence in the citizens of the United States. The idea of a "melting pot" society, where immigrant cultures are gradually absorbed by the American Dream, succumbed to the realization that cultural diversity is one of the strong points of contemporary American society. Being a hyphenated American is now in vogue. As such, being Portuguese-American is just as acceptable as Italian-American, Irish-American or any one of the hundred other variations.

For much of the past 200 hundred years, the United States and the Azores have had a symbiotic relationship: Azoreans provided unskilled labor for the U.S. economy and the United States served as an escape valve for the overpopulated islands. The particular nature of that relationship has constantly changed over time. New England whalers relied heavily upon Azorean peasants for their crews from 1840 through the 1880s and, in the process, transported thousands of young men from their homeland to the developing United States. The new immigrants found employment in the fishing fleets of New England and the farms of California. Settlement patterns in the initial stage of Portuguese migration to the United States, which were concentrated on the East and West Coasts, clearly reflected the influence of whaling and the attraction of the California Gold Rush. Most of those early immigrants left a rural environment in the islands to settle in rural areas or small towns in the United States.

During the second stage of migration from the 1870s to the 1920s, Portuguese immigrants continued to settle in concentrated communities in a few states. A difference developed, however, between the East and West Coasts in occupational opportunities and subsequent settlement patterns. Industrializing New England needed factory workers and Portuguese immigrants on the East Coast, for the most part, became urban industrial workers and provided unskilled labor for the textile mills. Portuguese women, who readily found employment in the mills, also contributed to a change in the nature and composition of the second stage of migration. In California, agriculture was still the major attraction during the early 1900s and many Azoreans eventually became independent farmers. The third major concentration of

Portuguese in America was a rather unique case. Originally brought into the Hawaiian Islands as contract agricultural workers, the Portuguese rapidly abandoned agriculture and moved to the urban areas.

The third major stage of Portuguese immigration began in the early 1960s and has continued until the present. Although still primarily concentrated in the same states, this stage is noticeably different from the previous ones and reflects the changing nature of both American and Portuguese society. California agriculture, transformed into a system of agribusiness, effectively eliminated the possibility of new immigrants becoming independent farmers. Service occupations in large urban centers replaced agriculture. Excluded from agriculture, a traditional occupation of Portuguese immigrants in the West, the percentage of new immigrants destined for California declined. In New England, the textile mills relocated to the South to take advantage of lower production costs and no longer provide traditional employment opportunities for large numbers of recent immigrants. Instead, large urban centers provide unskilled service jobs and employment opportunities for immigrants and natives alike. The appearance of a new core area of settlement for Portuguese immigrants on the periphery of New York City also reflects shifts in regionally-specific economic opportunities.

Two characteristics of the Portuguese migrations to the United States have contributed to the retention of traditional Azorean cultural practices and the maintenance of a sense of ethnic identity amongst immigrants: their concentrated settlement patterns, and the more-or-less continuous cultural reinforcement through new immigration. The patterns of settlement within a small number of counties in only a few states is largely attributable to the historical context of the initial stage of immigration and to effective social networks maintained between Portuguese communities in the United States and the Islands. Those networks were instrumental in encouraging new immigrants to join their friends and relatives already living in the United States and assisted them in securing housing and employment. In spite of the evolving nature of the relationship between the United States and the Azores as the United States has become both industrialized and urbanized, these social networks have continued to function effectively.

With the exception of one thirty-year interruption when Portuguese migration to the United States was almost non-existent, since the first

5

*by the racist
Quota Acts
of the 1920s,
promoted by
eugenicists.*

6

departures in the early 1820s there has been a consistent flow of Azorean immigrants into the United States. The migration increased dramatically from 1890 to 1920, only to be shut off by restrictive immigration legislation in the United States. The flood of migration that resumed in the mid-1960s brought an impressive number of Portuguese immigrants to this country in a short period of time. The arrival of large numbers of new immigrants and their concentration in areas already occupied by earlier Portuguese immigrants reinforced traditional cultural values and practices in those Portuguese communities. However, the cultural values of more recent immigrants are not necessarily the same as those of their predecessors. On the whole, recent immigrants are better educated and have a stronger sense of being Portuguese. Their arrival also coincides with an ethnic revitalization and growing sense of pride in one's ethnic heritage in the United States. In the past, cultural retention has remained strongest in the rural areas of California and, conversely, acculturation has been most pronounced in urban settings. The impact of the current immigration, which is directed almost exclusively to the larger urban areas, on cultural retention and the rate of acculturation among new Portuguese immigrants remains to be seen.

Migration has traditionally been a solution for human problems. When, for one reason or another, conditions have become unbearable in a particular location and appeared to be significantly better in another, the reaction has been to leave the one for the other. In that sense, migration is timeless; it is, in truth, a story without an end. The characters change from generation to generation, depending upon the specific motivations for a particular migration and the availability of a viable alternative, but the plot remains basically the same—an attempt to improve the political, economic or social well-being of a people by moving to a new location. In many ways, then, migration is a non-confrontational solution to human problems; in spite of the trauma of dislocation and personal adjustment, for some, migration is preferable to trying to bring about change within the native setting. Change, however, is one of the invariable consequences of migration. Conditions are modified in the homeland, in a variety of ways, by the departure of large numbers of the population. There is also, of course, a discernible impact on the receiving society. New populations, accompanied by their traditions and cultural values, adjust to life in the new homeland

and, in the process, modify their new homeland to reflect who and where they are. Sometimes these changes are readily observable; other times one has to look more intently to fully appreciate the impact of a particular migration.

For the last 180 years, then, these former residents of nine small Atlantic islands have been making their way to the United States and now, increasingly, to Canada. Their numbers fluctuated in response to conditions in both their old homeland and the new. They continued to come, however, and their coming has had a substantial impact on life in the Azores and in the areas where they settled in the United States. To appreciate the effects of this migration, it is necessary to start even before these first individuals made their long journey and carefully trace the chain of events from that time to the present.

7

Notes

[1] I am using George DeVos' definition of an ethnic group as "A self-perceived group of people who hold in common a set of traditions not shared by the others with whom they are in contact." In George DeVos, "Ethnic Pluralism: Conflict and Accommodation," *Ethnic Identity: Cultural Continuities and Change,* George DeVos and Lola Romanucei-Ross, eds. (Palo Alto: Mayfield, 1975), 9.

CHAPTER I

EMIGRATION: A RESPONSE TO ADVERSITY AND OPPORTUNITY

Behind the precipitous cliff coasts commonly found throughout the Azores are silent reminders of the volcanic activity that created these islands—enormous craters of extinct or dormant volcanoes, areas of bubbling mud pots and thermal springs, ancient lava-flows weathered by vegetation and climate, the still unweathered scars of historically recent lava-flows, and the almost 8,000-foot towering volcano that constitutes virtually all of the island of Pico and serves as the landmark for the archipelago. Tree-covered hills, rock-strewn fields and a scarcity of flat land are combined with a humid but mild climate to create a picturesque setting for the visitor, but an environment that necessitates diligence and hard work on the part of the inhabitants. Both elevation and relief restrict the use of that land, and agriculture is limited to the relatively flat areas below 1,000 feet, with pasture, forest and rough land occupying the rest. Settlements and roads, virtually all along the coast, and other uses compete with agriculture for the useable lowlands.[1]

In the early 15th century, when the Portuguese first discovered these uninhabited islands in the middle of the Atlantic, they provided a sufficient resource base for a modest agrarian population (see Map 2). Although the amount of level land was limited, the soil was rich, precipitation was adequate,[2] and the slopes were covered with forest. Lacking any other raw materials, the early inhabitants were forced to rely upon the soil and they quickly developed a system of agriculture adapted to their environment. To clear the rock-strewn fields, they built stone walls which also served to mark property lines; the forested slopes provided charcoal for fuel, and the cleared land was ideal for pasture. Lacking good harbors, they relied on small boats to fish the surround-

MAP 2

AZORES, DETAIL

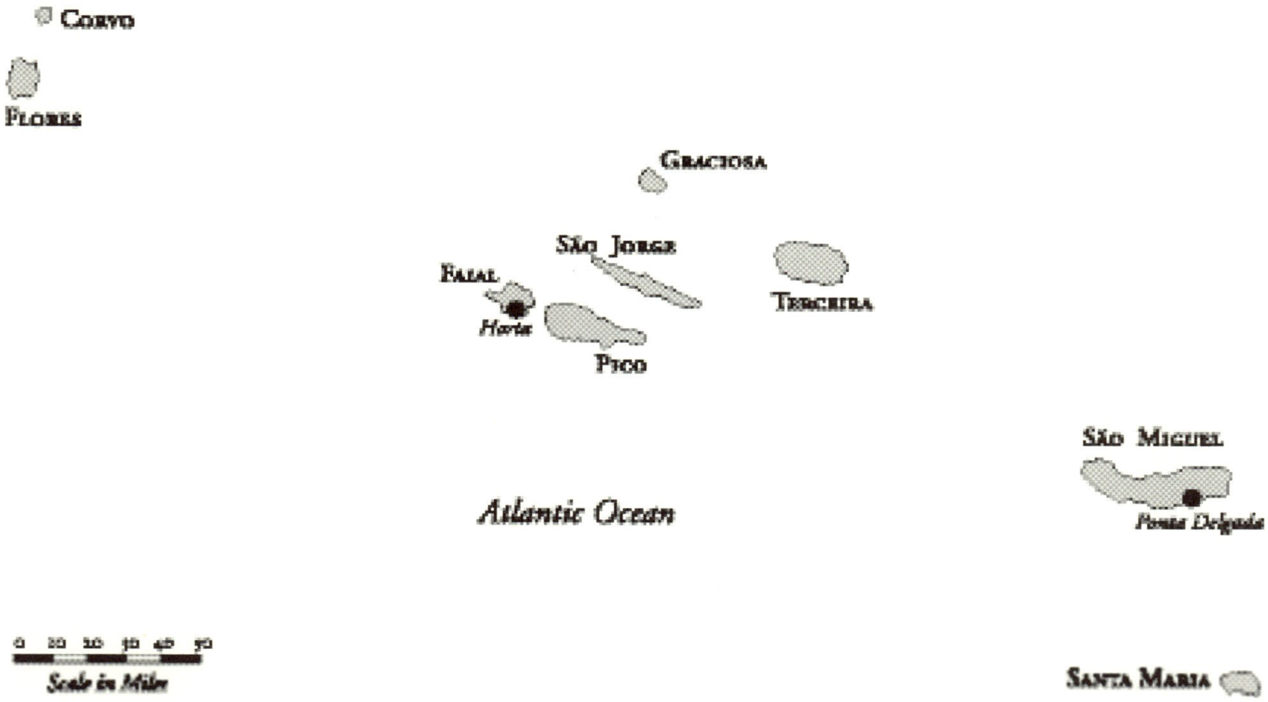

CORVO

FLORES

GRACIOSA

SÃO JORGE

TERCEIRA

FAIAL

Horta

PICO

SÃO MIGUEL

Ponta Delgada

Atlantic Ocean

SANTA MARIA

0   10   20   30   40   50
Scale in Miles

ing waters to supplement their diet. In short, the early settlers developed a survival technique well-suited to their particular environment.

Boom, Bust, and Survival

Few people, however, are satisfied with just surviving, particularly those who underwrote the expense of sending colonists to develop and exploit land given to them by the crown of Portugal. The elusive search for a rewarding cash crop suitable to these islands began with the first settlers in the 15th century and is still being sought today. In many ways, the economic history of the Azores is reminiscent of Brazil's, which was also settled by the Portuguese. In both cases, the inhabitants came to depend upon a particular crop or product which dominated the economy, only to see it eventually collapse due to competition from abroad or a decline in productivity and be slowly replaced by another product, which repeated the cycle. By developing its enormous deposits of mineral wealth, Brazil finally escaped the repetitious cycles of a "boom and bust" economy in the 20th century; but in the Azores the search continues. In the process, some of the plants and animals imported from all over the world proved beneficial, others disastrous, but each has had an impact on the islands.

One of the first cash crops to be introduced was sugar cane, but it quickly gave way to the woad plant, an important source of blue dye in the 15th and 16th centuries. By the mid-17th century, indigo from North America captured the world dye market and displaced woad. Wheat and flax were temporary substitutes, but wheat is an extensive crop requiring large areas to produce in any quantity and flax was most valuable for export after it had been processed into linens. Neither provided a satisfactory cash crop ideally suited to the environments found in these islands. Citrus and wine grapes were both important in the mid-18th century. England was the destination of most of the fruit grown in the Azores. From 1747 until 1838, lemons were one of the major products, until England found a better supply of lemons elsewhere and the market collapsed. By this time oranges had also become a very important export crop. In 1802 nearly 40,000 boxes of oranges were shipped to London alone and by the 1870s some 500,000 boxes, each containing from 300 to 400 oranges, were annually sent to the English market just from São Miguel.[3]

11

Hardy plants by nature, grapevines were a logical choice for plant-
ing in rocky soils unsuitable for cultivation or pastures. But successful
cultivation of wine grapes in the islands required a considerable input
of ingenuity and hard work. For the grapes to mature with a sufficient
sugar content to make good wine, vineyards needed to be protected
from the strong winds characteristic of the Azores. Removing the surface stones from even the rockiest areas usually uncovered sufficient soil
to plant the vines. These stones were then converted into walls to provide a windbreak and row after row of small, irregular- shaped cubicles,
often encasing no more than one hundred square feet with stone walls
three-to-four feet high, gradually spread over the rocky lowlands.
Viewed from the nearby hills, these vineyards created a very distinctive
maze-like pattern on the land. Once the technique was perfected, it
spread throughout the islands and wine became an increasingly important cash crop. By 1850, the island vineyards were annually producing
50,000 pipes of very good wine.[4]

In the continuing search for new cash crops, pineapples were introduced in the 1860s, and by the mid-1880s more than 125,000 pineapples a year were being exported to England. However, pineapples in the
Azores are a capital-intensive crop requiring hothouses and intensive
care. Initially introduced into the Ponta Delgada area of São Miguel,
they are still grown there today but never spread to other areas. In
1878, tea was introduced as a new commercial crop.[5] Ideally suited for
growing on the hilly uplands, enough tea is still produced on São
Miguel to satisfy the islands' needs and for export to mainland
Portugal. However, tea grown here could not compete with tea grown
in the Far East and another plan fizzled.

Every new crop, introduced to the islands with the expectation that
it would prove to be a valuable cash crop and an asset to the local economy, had a particular impact on the local environment. Some, such as
potatoes, beans and corn became the mainstay of the population and
spread throughout the islands. Others, such as tobacco, depleted the
soil and used up some of the best land. Still others, like oranges, made
their demands upon the environment in more indirect ways. Shipping
hundreds of thousands of boxes of oranges from the Azores to England
in the period from 1800 to 1880 required substantial quantities of
wood for fruit boxes. The gradual deforestation of the islands in search

of box wood hastened in times of crises when alternate supplies were restricted or cut off. By the late 1830s desperate orange exporters were "forced to cut down every available tree they could procure."[6] After most of the useable timber had been removed from the islands to make fruit boxes, fast-growing trees such as the Japanese cedar, eucalyptus from Australia, the acacia tree, and several varieties of pine were introduced from various parts of the world to try to satisfy the demand for wood. Some of these new species, however, had unforeseen detrimental effects on the environment. *Pittosporum*, for example, introduced from Australia in the 1840s to serve as a windbreak for oranges, enabled citrus orchards to expand into less favorable parts of the islands but also exhausted the soil.[7]

13

On all of the islands, a major portion of the agricultural land was devoted to subsistence crops to feed the local population, but a system of specialization, based upon the characteristics of each island, gradually evolved in the archipelago. São Miguel, the only island with a substantial amount of good agricultural land, was always in the forefront of the search for a remunerative cash crop. Almost all of the commercial crops—tobacco, tea, pineapples, and sugar cane—were introduced to that island first and most were never even marginally successful elsewhere. São Miguel was also the major producer of citrus fruit in the 18th and 19th centuries. Neither Terceira nor São Jorge possessed much good agricultural land, but both were well suited to raising cattle and became noted early for their cattle and dairy products. Faial and Pico, the two geographically closest yet physically dissimilar islands, developed a complementary system of agriculture. Diversified farming, including the cultivation of fruits, vegetables and grains was common on Faial. Pico, the second largest island, has very little land suited for general agriculture. Much of the rocky lowlands was converted to vineyards, and livestock were raised on the uplands. Graciosa and, to a lesser degree, Santa Maria developed vineyards to complement their subsistence agriculture. Flores and Corvo, among the smallest and most isolated islands, enjoyed even less favorable circumstances than the other seven islands, and their populations have always been preoccupied with subsistence agriculture.[8]

When the New England whalers began stopping in the Azores for fresh supplies at the beginning of the 19th century, the islands were no longer in their natural state. Small villages dotted the coastline and the land suitable for agriculture had already been intensively farmed for over 300 years. Livestock grazed on the slopes that were once heavily wooded but had long since been exploited for fuel and useable timber. The variety of foodstuffs available from the islands, in conjunction with an excellent harbor, soon made Horta, Faial the main Azorean port of call for the whaling vessels.

Social Hierarchy

In addition to their farming techniques, the early Portuguese settlers brought with them a system of land tenure that, in effect, relegated the masses to the permanent status of landless agricultural workers. Under this system, known as the perpetual leasehold, the tenant farmer paid his rent either in kind, when the crop was harvested, or in cash at the end of the year. The amount of rent was fixed, however, and not alterable.[9] Unlike sharecropping, where the landowner and tenant share in both the good years and the bad, in this system of land tenure the risks were all assumed by the tenant. An unusually good harvest benefited the tenants, but a crop failure could be devastating. Even worse, though, was the difficulty encountered by each tenant family's offspring in finding land to farm. In 1840, the agricultural land in the islands was controlled by less than three percent of the total population.[10] The leases that most of the tenants had on the land were hereditary, but they could not be sub-divided without the consent of the owner.[11] The number of people who not only did not own land, but could not even find land to farm, increased with each generation.

Nineteenth-century life in the Azores was the product of over 300 years of struggling to make a living from the soil in an isolated environment. A rigid social structure pervaded the lifestyle of the villages and exacerbated the lack of economic opportunity and upward mobility. Like most agrarian societies, the daily routine of life seldom changed and, in fact, was passed on from generation to generation. Children were born, raised, and eventually died in the village of their birth; and, while an individual's virtues were well-known throughout the village, so were his vices. Even so, the individual knew exactly who he was and where he fit into the social and economic life of his island.

He might not like his position in life or his general inability to change it, but there was no such thing as an identity crisis. In times of stress, the extended family, aided by an intricate and reciprocal system of god-parentage, could always be relied upon for assistance.

Living in the same village generation after generation eventually resulted in an extended family system whereby virtually everyone in the village was related in one way or another. Within this close-knit society, the individual identified most clearly with his particular village and the island on which it was located. Little, if any, thought was given to the fact that these islands, collectively known as the Azores, were considered by the Portuguese crown to be an integral part of Portugal or that the inhabitants were Portuguese citizens.

Compulsory military service for all young males was a persistent and unpopular burden of Portuguese citizenship for the Azoreans. At the age of sixteen, every male faced the prospects of eight years of military service in mainland Portugal.[12] This obligation weighed particularly heavy upon the peasant class. Although it was common practice to hire a substitute to serve the military duty, in reality this was an option available only to families with sufficient wealth to hire a substitute. As one observer noted in the 1880s, "The Azorean islander flies from the recruiting sergeant as he would from the Evil One, and, to escape service will run any risks..."[13] One of the options to military service which presented itself in the 19th century was to ship out as a common sailor on an American whaling vessel. Many young Azoreans peasants, with no sailing experience, took advantage of the option. Since it was illegal for young men to leave the islands without making a monetary payment to hire a substitute for military service, most of these departures were of a clandestine nature.

Overpopulation and Adversity

Like all agrarian societies, the Azoreans were dependent upon the soil for their survival and although there were occasional crop failures, as there are in any agricultural society, the surpluses and shortages tended to balance out. By the 19th century, however, these nine islands, which were clearly capable of providing a satisfactory life for a modest number of people, were seriously overpopulated. The normal vicissitudes of

15

Milton Silvia. Azorean village, no date.
Spinner Publications, Inc.

Miguel Corte-Real. Rural Women.
Santa Maria, Azores, no date.

an agrarian economy became fraught with anxiety as hunger more frequently accompanied crop failure. As one observer recorded, "when there is a scarcity, which is the case sometimes, it is not because the islands are unproductive, but because they are overloaded with population, and the crops are injured by incessant rains or strong winds."[14]

The first official Census of Portugal in 1864 documented what had long been apparent—the pressure on the limited amount of agricultural land had become intense.[15] Although the official population density ranged from a high of 398 persons per square mile on Faial to a low of 131 on Corvo, the real density was much higher. Population densities are calculated by dividing the total population by the total land area and, in the Azores, much of that land was unusable. With less than forty percent of the surface area of these islands suitable for agriculture, the average population density for this land was closer to 700 persons per square mile in 1864.[16] The Azorean peasant became adept at intensive agriculture on a very small scale. Yet, even good farmers occasionally get poor yields, and there is an absolute limit to the number of people a subsistence economy can sustain.

Adversity, an infrequent visitor to these islands prior to 1850, became a constant companion after the 1870s. The orange blight, which was accidentally introduced into the islands in 1835, gradually spread from island to island and appeared in São Miguel, the center of orange production, in 1877. By the mid-1880s, the citrus crop had declined to less than one-third of what it had been in 1870.[17] The arrival of two other plant diseases to the Azores in the early 1850s also caused great consternation and hastened the departure of many young men to the California gold fields. The first of these was a potato rot that struck at the very heart of the islanders' diet. Potatoes, the principal subsistence crop, were grown on all the islands and the effects of the potato rot were widely felt. It was followed, in 1853, by a deadly fungus, *Oidium tuckeii*, which struck the grapevines in the islands and rapidly spread with disastrous results throughout the archipelago.[18] It established such a pervasive grip on the crop that it was not brought under control until the mid-20th century when new methods of combating it were introduced.[19] Wine production declined precipitously; "proprietors who used to have one thousand barrels of wine yearly, … some seasons, [had] scarcely thirty."[20] Wine production, though found on almost all the islands, was heavily concentrated on Pico and to a lesser extent on Graciosa. The loss of their vineyards thus struck the inhabitants of Pico particularly hard, especially because the serious deficit of agricultural land made it impossible to switch to other crops. Accompanying the devastating drop in commercial production was a comparable decline in subsistence crops. An 1886 account of the islands noted that, "In 1876-77, there commenced that general failure of crops, which has recurred every year with more or less intensity to the present time, causing a complete stagnation in trade, and reducing numbers of families dependent upon the produce of their lands to considerable straits."[21]

Few alternatives to farming existed in the islands. The New England whalers offered an escape from the hand-to-mouth existence of subsistence farming and the obligation to serve in the Portuguese military. Pico's proximity to and association with Faial gave these islanders ample opportunity to join the whaleships calling at Horta, Faial. An initial attempt to introduce shore-whaling to the island of Faial in 1832 was unsuccessful, but conditions had changed by the early 1850s and the second effort succeeded. Shore-whaling for sperm whales, employing the same techniques that were used along the New England coast in the 17th century, gradually spread to the other islands, but Pico and Faial dominated whaling in the Azores.[22] The men of Pico acquired the reputation of fearless whalers, both in the islands and on board the New England whaleships, and that reputation is still widely known and maintained in the islands today. Shore-whaling never provided an adequate livelihood for a substantial number of Azoreans, however, and throughout the islands men were forced to turn elsewhere to earn a living.

Emigration

The people of the Azores responded to their misfortunes as best they could. Like people everywhere in times of trouble, they worked harder although to little or no avail, borrowed money from their more fortunate relatives and friends and, when all else failed, began to consider the alternative of leaving their homeland. The occasional departee of the early 1800s was replaced by a steady trickle of men in the 1820s and a flowing stream of escapees by 1840. Emigration dramatically increased as conditions deteriorated and the population of the islands slowly but

23

steadily mounted during the last three decades of the 19th century. In the fifty years between 1870 and 1920, in what is known as the second stage of emigration, the "pull" of the United States became irresistible and several hundred thousand Azoreans joined the millions of Europeans who left for the New World in search of a better life. During the following three decades marked by economic depression, World War, and rising xenophobia in the United States, emigration almost ceased. Only in the 1960s, the beginning of the third stage of emigration, did Azoreans once again begin leaving for the United States and Canada in significant numbers.

The government of Portugal, seemingly oblivious to conditions on the islands and, no doubt, preoccupied with events elsewhere, did not make the decision to emigrate any easier. Cognizant of the ever-increasing number of emigrants who were trying to escape an apparently hopeless existence and ever watchful to ensure a continuous supply of military conscripts, the Portuguese government passed a law in April, 1873, whereby "monetary payment in substitution of enlistment was abolished, and the unhappy emigrate was still liable to be called upon to serve, if he returned prior to attaining his 36th year."[23] However, it soon became apparent to the government that without being permitted to provide a substitute for military service, young men would surreptitiously leave the country and not return, thereby inflicting a double loss to the country—the disappearance of a worker whose product might be taxed and the absence of a potential military conscript. The government quickly moved to rectify its error and in 1880 passed a law compelling all males, when they reached the age of fourteen, to deposit the equivalent of $42 to the State before they would be permitted to leave the country. Should the emigrant not return to serve his military duty, the money would be used to hire a substitute.[24] Laws have always been easier to enact than they are to enforce and this one was no exception. In 1886, it was noted that "Emigration, generally clandestine, has of late years greatly relieved the necessitous condition of these poor islanders" even though "the difficulties in the way of the over-plus population seeking their fortune elsewhere have been increased."[25]

After years of thwarting the law, the alternatives sometimes become as institutionalized as the laws themselves. When, in 1903, for example, a boy from Pico finally persuaded his father to let him emigrate to

America, to join his sister in New Bedford, clandestine departures were still common practice.

> Because of my age, fifteen, the government would not give me a pass-
> port. The government wanted the boys to wait until they were eight-
> een, then go to serve in the army for two or three years. My father had
> to pay an agent to smuggle me out of the Azores. The agents were pro-
> fessional smugglers. They operated regular services, for which young
> men paid a fee in order to get out of the islands.[26]

In this instance, no fewer than twenty-two other young men were smuggled out in the same boat. Although illegal emigrants could be apprehended by a Portuguese revenue cutter and returned to face a heavy fine, the likelihood was extremely slim. Consequently, many young men were willing to risk leaving the islands to search for greater opportunities elsewhere.

25

The Azores were not alone with their problems of declining agricultural productivity and increasing population. Similar conditions existed throughout Portugal, including the mainland, Cape Verde, and Madeira and the inhabitants of many of Portugal's regions sought new opportunities elsewhere. Portuguese citizens were fortunate, in one way, during the 19th and 20th centuries, in that several options were open to them. They could migrate elsewhere within the Portuguese colonial empire, such as to Mozambique or to Angola in Africa, or to Brazil, a former colony that gained independence in 1888. Moving to a Portuguese-speaking country with similar customs made the transition easier than going to a completely foreign country such as the United States.

Between 1890 and 1921, official records indicate that of the approximately one million Portuguese who emigrated from their homeland only sixteen percent were destined for America.[27] The vast majority of emigrants were from the mainland and their destination was overwhelmingly (eighty-five percent) to Brazil. Only about five percent of the mainland Portuguese ended up in the United States. The others went either to Europe or Africa. The Madeira Islands, with much smaller numbers of emigrants during these years, were primarily oriented to Brazil, where more than half of their out-migration was directed, and to a lesser degree to the United States and Hawaii, where a little more than a third of the remaining emigrants ended up.[28] Emigrants leaving Cape Verde went almost exclusively to the United States and their story is quite distinct from that of other Portuguese.[29] Of the recorded emigration from the Azores, eighty-two percent chose to go to the United States, sixteen percent selected Brazil and the balance was lightly scattered between Europe and Africa. Within the islands, there was considerable variation from district to district: from the District of Horta (Pico, Faial, Flores, and Corvo) ninety-four percent emigrated to the United States and five percent went to Brazil; from the District of Ponta Delgada (São Miguel and Santa Maria) eighty-four percent selected the United States and fourteen percent chose Brazil; from the District of Angra (Terceira, São Jorge, and Graciosa) the percentages were sixty-eight and thirty-one respectively.[30]

26

One estimate of the origin of Portuguese emigrants bound for the United States in the years 1892-1912 concluded that sixty-three percent were from the Azores, twenty-six percent from mainland Portugal, and about eleven percent from the Madeira Islands.[31] Within the United States, there are also significant regional differences. The Portuguese in California are, for example, almost exclusively of Azorean descent and primarily from five of the nine islands—Pico, Faial, Flores, São Jorge and Terceira. The Portuguese immigrants to Hawaii were primarily from the Madeira Islands and the island of São Miguel in the Azores. Emigrants from Cape Verde have tended to settle in southeastern Massachusetts, specifically around the whaling port of New Bedford. Emigrants from São Miguel remained almost exclusively on the East Coast, particularly in Massachusetts, Rhode Island, and Connecticut, as did those from mainland Portugal and the Madeira Islands. Most studies have estimated that Azoreans constitute somewhere between two-thirds and three-fourths of all Portuguese in the United States.[32] The following account thus aims to contribute to our understanding of Portuguese-Americans by focusing on the Azorean portion of this story.

Notes

[1] Area and General Elevation of the Azores

	Area in Sq. Miles	% Below 1,000 Feet	% Above 1,000 Feet
Santa Maria	37	86.4	13.6
São Miguel	288	52.7	47.3
Terceira	153	55.6	44.4
Graciosa	24	94.5	5.7
São Jorge	92	30.1	69.9
Pico	168	41.2	58.8
Faial	66	53.5	46.5
Flores	55	32.5	67.5
Corvo	6.7	45.1	54.9
TOTAL	889.7		

SOURCE: *Açores : Do 25 de Abril até aos nossos dias*, 150.

[2] From about 50 inches of rain falls annually on Flores to about 35 inches per year on Santa Maria.

[3] Walter Walker, *The Azores or Western Islands: A Political, Commercial and Geographical Account* (London, 1886), 86.

[4] Ibid., 91. A pipe was a unit of measure equivalent to two hogsheads - each of which contained 63 gallons. Each pipe of wine then was approximately 125 gallons.

[5] Ibid., 91-96.

[6] Ibid., 101.

[7] Ibid., 91-99.

[8] A.R. Graves, "Immigrants in Agriculture: The Portuguese Californians, 1850-1970s" (Ph.D. dissertation, University of California, Los Angeles), 34-38.

[9] Walker, *The Azores or Western Islands*, 78-79.

[10] Graves, "Immigrants in Agriculture," 34.

[11] Walker, *The Azores or Western Islands*, 79.

[12] Berger, J. *In Great Waters: The Story of Portuguese Fishermen* (New York, 1941), 45-46.

[13] Walker, *The Azores or Western Islands*, 111-12.

[14] Borges de F. Henriques, *A Trip to the Azores or Western Islands* (Boston, 1867), 30.

[15] **AREA, POPULATION AND DENSITY OF THE AZORES, 1865**

Islands	Area in Sq. Miles	Population per Sq. Mile	Persons per Island
Santa Maria	37	5,863	158
São Miguel	288	105,404	366
Terceira	153	45,781	300
Graciosa	24	8,718	366
São Jorge	92	17,998	195
Pico	168	27,721	165
Faial	66	26,259	398
Flores	55	10,259	191
Corvo	6.7	883	131
TOTAL	889.7	249,135	280

SOURCE: *Súmula de Dados Estatísticos* (Açores: Departmento Regional de Estudos e Planeamento, 1976), 4.

[16] Ibid., 2.

[17] Walker, *The Azores or Western Islands,* 88-91.

[18] Ibid., 91.

[19] R. Clarke, "'Open Boat Whaling in the Azores' (The History and Present Methods of a Relic Industry)," *Discovery Reports,* 26: 77.

[20] Borges de Henriques, *A Trip to the Azores or Western Islands,* 31-32.

[21] Walker, *The Azores or Western Islands,* 77.

[22] Clarke, "Open Boat Whaling in the Azores," 352.

[23] Walker, *The Azores or Western Islands,* 112.

[24] Ibid., 107.

[25] Ibid., 107.

[26] L. Oliver, *Never Backward: The Autobiography of Lawrence Oliver—A Portuguese-American* (San Diego, 1972), 10.

[27] Prior to about 1900, official records of the number of emigrants leaving Portugal, including the Azores, are virtually nonexistent and emigration records, at best, give only a general indication of the scale of the migration that took place at the end of the 19th and beginning of the 20th century. After 1900, the records are incomplete with entire years unaccounted for or only partially recorded. What records do exist are for legal departures only and do not include the unofficial emigrants who, by all accounts, comprised a substantial number from the Azores as well as from the mainland. The records are even worse when used to determine precise points of origin. Even the decennial censuses of the United States, which are the most accurate source of information on the number of foreign-born Portuguese residing in this country, at least through 1960, provide little useful information on whether the Portuguese immigrant came from the Azores or the mainland. In the earlier censuses, 1870-1900, a separate category for the Atlantic Islands included part of the Azoreans, depending upon whether the census enumerator listed that as a separate category or, more typically, included Azoreans under Portugal. In more recent years, 1930 for example, the Azores were listed as a separate category, although the majority of Azoreans were usually grouped under the category of Portugal.

[28] Graves, "Immigrants in Agriculture," 42.

[29] Early Cape Verdean emigration to the United States also followed the geography of whaling and the largest and earliest settlements were around the whaling center of New Bedford. Immigrant settlements are primarily in southeastern Massachusetts. They subsequently gained ownership of their own means of transportation and immigrants came to the U.S. largely on packet ships owned by Cape Verdeans. They are the only African immigrants to come to the New World as free men and women. Until 1975, Cape Verdeans were Portuguese citizens and counted as "Portuguese" in census reports. After 1975, Cape Verde achieved independence from Portugal and immigrants from the islands were counted as "Cape Verdean."

[30] Walker, *The Azores or Western Islands,* 107-108. Although incomplete, these records substantiate general observations made concerning the destination of Azorean emigrants as early as the 1880s. "The stream of emigration from the three most eastern islands of São Miguel, Santa Maria and Terceira, has through accidental circumstances generally proceeded steadily to Brazil, whereas that from the western most islands of Faial, São Jorge and Flores is directed mainly to the United States, whilst Madeira, singularly enough, contributes a by no means insignificant quota to the Sandwich Islands ...."

[31] Graves, "Immigrants in Agriculture," 89.

[32] Ibid., 89.

CHAPTER II

THE NEW ENGLAND HABIT

Slow Boat to America—The Initial Wave of Emigration

There is no surviving account of when the first individual left the Azores for "America," which is probably just as well since many of the early departees left clandestinely and preferred that their leaving not be noted. It is clear, though, that the first significant migration from the Azores to the United States, its territories and future constituent parts occurred between 1800 and 1870. The impetus for the initial departures was as much the "pull" from America, in the form of jobs on whaling ships that were plying their trade in Azorean waters, as it was the "push" from a very traditional society isolated on nine small islands with little to offer its young inhabitants. During this period, the New England whalers provided the initial jobs and means of transportation to those seeking to leave the island. It was also the geography of the whaling industry that first established the very concentrated settlement of Portuguese immigrants in California, coastal New England, and Hawaii.

Massachusetts dominated the whaling industry among the American colonies from the beginning with the early centers of Nantucket and Cape Cod gradually being supplanted by New Bedford in the late 1700s.[1] By the early 19th century, New Bedford had become the center of whaling in America.[2] During this period, the fleet expanded its work from the traditional whaling grounds in the Atlantic to explore the seemingly endless possibilities in the Pacific, and San Francisco and Hawaii became major ports of call. It had, however, by the early 1800s become increasingly difficult to find enough crewmen to man the growing whaling fleet. Instead of receiving a set wage, the crew of the whaler participated in a form of profit sharing called the lay system.[3]

While this system proved to be quite lucrative for the owners of the ships and usually rewarding for the officers and primary crewmembers, the common sailor frequently had little to show at the conclusion of a lengthy and often difficult voyage. Shipping out on a whaler did not offer the same attraction that it had a half-century earlier, and other opportunities on the expanding western frontier proved more attractive to many of the young men in the United States.

It thus became common practice to obtain Americans for the ships' principal officers and sign on the remainder of the crew wherever they could be found. One place where they were easily recruited was the Azores. The waters in the vicinity of the islands were a feeding ground for sperm whales and the New Englanders had become well-acquainted with the islands in their pursuit of these whales. Some 2,000 miles east of Massachusetts, 700 miles off the coast of Portugal and 750 miles from Africa, they are the only island chain in the mid-Atlantic and ideally situated as a stopping point for outward-bound whalers desiring to replenish their supplies before heading for the southern fishery. (see Map 1). From Flores, the most westerly island, the archipelago extends along a northwest-southeast line some 375 miles to Santa Maria, the most southeasterly island[4] (see Map 2). A rugged, inhospitable shoreline greeted the New England whalers when they reached the Azores, and in the nine islands only Horta, Faial and Ponta Delgada, São Miguel had protected harbors. These two became regular ports of call for many of the Atlantic whalers, both as a source of fresh provisions and as a depot and trans-shipment point for whale oil and bones.

What began as a small number of Azoreans signing on as crew on the whalers in the 1820s, rapidly increased as the whaling fleet continued to expand in the 1840s and '50s and living conditions in the islands deteriorated. As Herman Melville noted in his novel, *Moby Dick*, which is based on his experience as a crewman on whaling vessels in the early 1840s, less than half of the seamen employed in the American whale fishery were Americans. They constituted virtually all of the officers, but most of the crewmen were recruited elsewhere. He observed that, "No small number of these whaling seamen belong to the Azores, where the outward bound Nantucket whalers frequently touch to augment their crews from the hardy peasants of those rocky shores."[5] The life of a seaman on an American whaling vessel with its deprivations, lengthy voyages and frequently meager rewards was certainly no easier for the Azoreans than it had been for the American sailors. Yet, they signed on in increasing numbers and proved themselves so well that they were soon "sought after by the masters for their daring pursuit of the fish, as well as for their quiet behavior on board."[6] Such accounts reveal a great deal about the nature of the people who inhabited these islands, but they also indicate that conditions there must have been very austere for so many young men to abandon their homeland for a life on board an American whaler.

The Azoreans quickly learned that whaling was a hard life, but so was the struggle to survive in their homeland. At the conclusion of each voyage, the whaling vessels returned to their homeport, which was almost always in Massachusetts and frequently the port of New Bedford. Once the catch was sold, the crew was paid and released and the ship was outfitted for a new cruise. After a short stay in port, most sailors shipped out on another voyage and continued as whalers in the 1820s and '30s. A few returned to the islands with tales to tell about the life of a whaler and this new country with unlimited land and great opportunities. Such stories must have made the bleak existence in the Azores seem even bleaker and many young men decided to try whaling as a viable alternative.

The initial voyage convinced some novice sailors that there must be a better way of earning a living than endlessly pursuing whales around the globe. For them the first voyage was also the last. Most often they ended up in Massachusetts, less frequently in California and occasionally in Hawaii. The Azores, however, had a surplus population, and there were always new recruits ready to take the places of their countrymen. With the expansion of the whaling fleet in the 1840s and 1850s, there was seldom any difficulty in finding a ship that needed crewmen. In the 1840s, the American whaleship was seen not only as an alternative itself to a difficult life in the islands, but also increasingly as a way to get to America. Granted, it was a slow voyage—two and three year cruises were not uncommon then—and it was a hard life. With any luck, though, an individual could end up in America without having spent any money for his passage and even have enough money from his share of the voyage to enable him to get settled.[7]

By 1870, the foundations had been well-established for the subsequent waves of out-migration from the Azores to the United States.

Azoreans were well settled in the coastal areas of Massachusetts, primarily around whaling centers such as New Bedford, and neighboring Providence, Rhode Island. In the twenty years between 1850 and 1870, California became the leading center of Portuguese settlement, and if gold mining had not proved to be lucrative, farming had. The men from the Azores continued to fill the ranks of the whaling fleet in the 1860s and 1870s and to a lesser extent, due to the decline of the industry, throughout the remainder of the century. Azoreans also manned shore whaling stations in various places around the world, prompting one authority on whaling to write that, "Afloat and ashore the islanders were ubiquitous in the nineteenth-century whaling scene"[8] (see Map 3). The practice of signing on a whaler to get free passage to America became an established tradition in the islands and brought the first Portuguese immigrants to New England, California and Hawaii.

Industrialization and Beginnings of the Second Stage

When the young immigrant from the Azores stepped ashore in New England in the early 1870s, his compatriots had already established themselves in a number of occupational niches and were, in effect, holding the doors open to fellow compatriots. The social network which was all pervasive in the islands also extended to family members living in the United States and it effectively spared most new immigrants from undue anxiety about their new life. For the most part, they joined members of their extended family or friends, either on a temporary or a more permanent basis, and relied heavily upon them for advice in finding jobs and arranging living accommodations. The existence of this effective social network between family members in the islands and the United States played a major role in determining where the post-1870 immigrants settled and strongly influenced the occupational opportunities available to them.[9]

At the beginning of the second stage in the migration of Azoreans to the United States, the 1870 census reported 8,971 Portuguese living in this country and its territories.[10] Although one or more Portuguese were reported in thirty-six of the thirty-seven states, most of the immigrant population was on either the East or West Coast and highly concentrated in and around a relatively small number of communities. Former whaling centers, such as New Bedford, Providence and New Haven, were the primary centers in Massachusetts, Rhode Island and Connecticut. With 2,555 Portuguese, Massachusetts accounted for thirty percent of the U.S. total and one out of every five of these immigrants (513) was living in Boston. The Portuguese population of New Bedford at about 800 was sufficiently large in 1867 to justify sending a Portuguese-speaking Catholic priest to care for them.[11] Fewer Portuguese were found in New York (334 - 4%), Connecticut (221 - 2.6%) and Rhode Island (189 - 2.2%), but these four states collectively contained thirty-six percent of the Portuguese population in 1870. The other major concentration of Portuguese in the United States was in California, where 3,435 Portuguese, forty percent of the U.S. total, were living primarily in the San Francisco Bay Area, one-time whaling port and entrance to the gold fields.[12]

After 1870, the bulk of the Portuguese immigrants relied on more traditional modes of transportation including packet ships,[13] cargo and passenger ships between Europe and the East Coast and finally, steamships operating directly between the Azores and New England for the exclusive purpose of transporting immigrants. The advertisements of these steamship companies promised fast, reliable service between the Azores and the United States. The volume of traffic was sufficient for the barkentine, *Moses B. Tower,* for example, to make four regular trips between New Bedford and the islands in 1889.[14] In 1911, the steamship *Venezia* was advertised as providing monthly service directly between the city of Angra, on the island of Terceira, and the United States. In addition to good accommodations, the company promised a voyage of only five-and-one-half days to the United States as well as rail transportation from the East Coast to California. Such arrangements were a far cry from the earlier period when men spent two or three years working their way to the United States on a whaling ship. The prospects of a relatively fast, pleasant trip to join family members already in America encouraged many who were inclined to emigrate yet reluctant to travel.

The pace of Portuguese immigration to the United States quickened steadily until 1900 and then escalated rapidly over the next twenty years. Sixty-two percent of all Portuguese immigrants who came to the United States between 1820 and 1930 arrived in the twenty years

Portuguese fishermen salting codfish, Provinceton, MA,
circa 1900. Spinner Publications, Inc.

Lewis Hine. Portuguese Spinner, Fall River, 1916.
Library of Congress.

Lewis Hine. Young workers in Cornell Mill,
Fall River, 1912. Library of Congress.

Lewis Hine. Recreational Meeting
of Portuguese Youth Group, Fall River, 1916.
Library of Congress.

between 1900 and 1920 (see Figure 1). As one immigrant commented about coming to the United States in 1903, "It was easy to get into this country in those early days. America was a free port. To get in, all you needed was a little money in your pocket, so that the authorities could be sure that you wouldn't be destitute and on relief right away."[15]

FIGURE I

PORTUGUESE IMMIGRATION TO THE UNITED STATES, 1870-1930

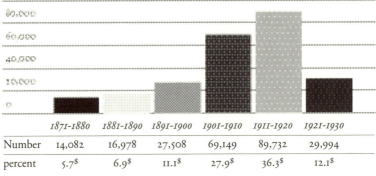

	1871-1880	1881-1890	1891-1900	1901-1910	1911-1920	1921-1930
Number	14,082	16,978	27,508	69,149	89,732	29,994
percent	5.7$	6.9$	11.1$	27.9$	36.3$	12.1$

SOURCE: IMMIGRATION NATURALIZATION SERVICE, 1976

Like immigrants the world over, the Portuguese coming to this country tended to be men and women in the prime of their lives. Seventy-three percent of the immigrants arriving between 1899 and 1917 were between fourteen and forty-four, twenty percent were under fourteen, while those forty-five and older accounted for only seven percent.[16] The Portuguese who came to America were not fleeing religious or political oppression. They were seeking to improve themselves economically and were willing and capable of working hard to achieve that aim. Letters from friends and relatives living in America vividly described the opportunities awaiting the individual willing to work. Those letters, together with the stories spun by returned emigrants, certainly exaggerated the possibilities for success and spurred the flow of new immigrants. It became "almost a habit" in the Azores to emigrate to the United States.[17]

In the early stages of Portuguese migration to the United States, immigrants were predominantly male. This was, in large part, a reflection of their unusual method of arriving in this country mainly as sailors on whaling vessels. By 1900, when the flow of immigrants had increased markedly and the mode of transportation had become more traditional, Azorean women also began coming to the United States in substantial numbers. Between 1900 and 1919, the ratio of male-to-female emigrants was approximately three to two.[18] There were no restrictions on women leaving their homeland as they were not subject to conscription and therefore not required to post a bond or resort to clandestine departures. The demand for female labor to work in the cotton mills of Fall River, New Bedford and Providence made it relatively easy for them to find employment. By 1900, there was a sufficiently large Portuguese population in those cities, and finding a relative or acquaintance to stay with was not a substantial problem. Some women came to the United States to marry their future husbands who had sent for them, while others came to join family members who had emigrated earlier. Once here, women were much less likely to return to their native islands than were men. For every woman who left the United States to return home between 1908 and 1919, three men also departed.[19]

Although the initial immigration process was virtually identical for Azoreans who settled on the East and West Coasts, there was a noticeable difference in the environments in which they found themselves. The East Coast of the United States was already well-settled when the main flow of Portuguese immigrants arrived and, as a consequence, the majority of the Azoreans who settled there made a rapid transition from their former rural lifestyle to a new urban-industrial way of life. The West Coast was far removed from the economic center of the nation at the turn of the century and offered decidedly different opportunities and experiences than those that characterized New England. Those differences have been reflected in the Portuguese population of the United States ever since.

Economic Opportunities—The Sea, the Land, and the Factory

There was no shortage of opportunities in the United States for the former whaler turned immigrant. As the economic activity in New Bedford demonstrated, there was much more to whaling than just chasing and killing whales. "With its oil refineries [whale oil], cooper's shops, tool-works, and the hundred-and-one industries subsidiary to whaling, New Bedford became a hive of industry...."[20] In 1857, the year that whaling reached its apogee, New Bedford alone had a fleet of 329 ships, worth more than twelve million dollars and manned by more than ten thousand seamen.[21] To maintain, outfit and supply these ships with the goods necessary to sustain them on a three or four year voyage was a monumental task requiring organizational expertise and strong backs. New England businessmen provided the former and many a reformed whaler furnished the latter. In addition to preparing the ships for departure, the whale oil and bone brought in by these vessels had to be processed into oil for lubrication or burning, medical ointments, candies, corset staves and dozens of other by-products. Although New Bedford was the principal whaling port in America, the same scene, on a reduced scale, was repeated in numerous other ports along the coast of Massachusetts.

46

For the islanders enamored of the sea but disenchanted with whaling, numerous other opportunities presented themselves. The cod and mackerel fisheries of Massachusetts were an important part of the 19th century economy and a natural choice for experienced fishermen no longer eager to undergo the trials of whaling. In 1855, the various ports in Massachusetts sent 1,138 ships, manned by 10,419 hands, to the cod and mackerel fisheries. Ten years later the number of men employed reached 11,358 and Cape Cod alone sent 314 ships and 3,832 men after these fish.[22] By the 1860s, when the whaling industry began its gradual but steady decline, a number of Portuguese whalers had worked their way to positions of authority. For these captains and officers who had known no other life but the sea, the cod and mackerel fisheries were a logical alternative to whaling and many took advantage of the opportunity.[23]

In addition to being the center of whaling and cod fishing, Massachusetts was also in the forefront of the coastal trade between the individual states and the deep water trade between various world ports. The port of Boston was second only to New York in commercial traffic and merchant ships vied with whalers and fishing vessels for crewmen. Low pay and less than ideal working conditions made it difficult to recruit seamen and "few Americans could be found in the forecastles of merchantmen on deep waters."[24] For the Azorean sailor, America thus provided no dearth of opportunities on the sea.

Among those who found life on the sea too harsh, some turned to farming. Azoreans had been raised in a traditional agrarian society and were, after all, first and foremost, farmers. The hinterland of New Bedford and nearby Providence, Rhode Island had been occupied and farmed for almost 250 years so that idle land suitable for farming was virtually non-existent. Farm laborers, not unlike sailors, typically worked long hours for low wages and dissatisfaction with life as a farmhand was almost as prevalent as it was among whalers. There were thus always jobs to be had as hired hands on local farms, and a number of young men from the Azores applied themselves to an occupation they already knew well. Skilled at squeezing a living from a small piece of land, some went on to become farmers themselves, first renting or working a small piece of land on a share basis and then gradually acquiring enough capital to purchase their own farms.

Massachusetts was more than ports and farmland in the 19th century; it was also at the heart of the industrial revolution sweeping across the United States. The rivers and streams that dropped down out of the hinterland to the sea were impossible to navigate but an excellent source of cheap power. These streams were harnessed, up and down the coast, to drive the machinery of industrial development. Cotton mills, where raw fibers were converted into finished materials, sprang into life all along this fall line in the early 1800s. The first cotton mill in Fall River, a port town between New Bedford and Providence, began production in 1813; sixty years later the textile mills in Fall River were employing in excess of 10,000 workers.[25] New Bedford, although preoccupied with whaling, eventually moved towards a more assured industrial base and its first cotton mill went into operation in 1849. Others followed, and by 1870 the city's four mills provided jobs for about two thousand industrial workers.[26]

In addition to cheap power to drive the machinery, industry in the mid-1800s required abundant supplies of unskilled labor, and immigrants, including the Portuguese, provided the poorly-paid unskilled labor force that industrialized the United States. Raised in a subsistence agrarian economy, the vast majority of the islanders were neither skilled nor educated. Textile mills are ideally suited for just such a work force; labor intensive by nature, few jobs required more than minimal training. To be a bobbin boy, doffer, carder, comber, sweeper, spooler or any one of the other numerous semi-skilled occupations involved in manufacturing material from fiber did not require understanding the principles of hydraulic power or the operation of a mechanical loom. All

47

that was necessary was to be able to stay awake and perform a tedious, repetitious task in an unpleasant environment for ten or twelve hours a day. The mills of New Bedford, Fall River and Providence seemed to have an insatiable demand for laborers and many Azoreans joined the ranks of the industrial workers. Few in number in the 1850s, Azorean mill workers gradually increased in the 1860s and 1870s and paved the way for their compatriots who poured into this area in subsequent decades. After 1890, the flow of Portuguese immigrants increased dramatically and their numbers alone forced them to seek employment in industries with more intensive labor demands characteristic of cotton mills and or related industries.

48

Settling in Massachusetts

Throughout the second stage of migration, the new immigrants, for the most part, chose as their destination those places where friends and relatives had already established themselves. Massachusetts was the ideal destination for many of the new immigrants: a sizeable Portuguese population already resided in the state; it was one of the easiest locations to get to from the Azores, which meant lower transportation costs; and employment opportunities were readily available. By 1900, Massachusetts had surpassed California with the largest Portuguese population in the country. Limited by their general lack of education and unfamiliarity with industrial machinery, the early Portuguese immigrants in Massachusetts were primarily concentrated in a relatively small number of occupational categories: whaling, fishing and sailing; farm laborers and small scale farmers; or, unskilled industrial workers in labor intensive mills. Whaling declined steadily after the 1870s, but it continued to be a viable occupation for a limited number of seamen. Seafaring jobs were much more likely in Provincetown and Gloucester where the fleets departed for the Grand Banks of Newfoundland in search of codfish and halibut. The greatest demand, however, was for men and women to work in the flourishing textile mills of Fall River, New Bedford, Taunton, Lowell, and Lawrence, and after 1890 the majority of the newcomers ended up in one of these mill towns.

Although the Census of 1870 did not record how many second-generation Portuguese were living in Massachusetts, the foreign-born

Portuguese population of the state was 2,555, many of whom had been residents of New Bedford for twenty years or more and undoubtedly had a number of children. Most of the Portuguese lived either in Bristol County, where both New Bedford and Fall River are located, or on nearby Cape Cod, especially in the fishing community of Provincetown at the tip of the Cape. They could also be found, to a lesser degree, scattered in the many fishing communities along the Massachusetts coast. The major fishing ports, such as Gloucester in the extreme northern part of the state, also had fairly substantial Portuguese populations.

The increased scarcity of whales and competition from petroleum products after 1870 resulted in a substantial decline in the whaling industry, but the impact was partially offset by an expansion in Banks fishing. The Grand Bankers, ships fitted out for a five or six month fishing voyage in search of codfish and halibut, derived their name from the Grand Banks of Newfoundland where they did most of their fishing. Provincetown was the center of Grand Banks fishing in Massachusetts and, as such, attracted many of the early Portuguese immigrants who came over between 1870 and 1890. In the Provincetown fleet, "most of the skippers were men from the Azores, and their countrymen kept coming over to fill up the crew lists."[27] The Grand Banks fleet reached its maximum expansion about 1885, but continued to be an important industry until after the turn of the century.

After 1880, Banks fishing was gradually superseded by a growing all-season fishing fleet that provided fresh fish for the urban centers of Boston and New York. Provincetown also took the lead in developing the fresh-fish fleet and Portuguese fisherman owned and operated many of the boats. The regular supply of fresh fish and connecting overnight rail service between Boston and New York gradually established the port of Boston as the center of the Atlantic fishery.[28] Portuguese continued to occupy an important role in the fishing fleets of Massachusetts in the 20th century, but the relative importance of fishing as an industry had long since been overshadowed by the industrial developments taking place within the state. By the second decade of the 20th century, it was noted that, "The Portuguese are still prominent in fishing and other sea-faring occupations, but their total number in these pursuits, though considerable, is not great when compared with those in the textile mills."[29]

49

New Bedford succeeded in transforming itself from the whaling center of the United States in the 1850s to a major textile manufacturing center with 2,600 workers employed in the cotton mills in 1889.[30] Even though wages for unskilled labor in the mills were low, jobs were easy to get and the pay was superior to many other unskilled jobs in the area. One sixteen-year-old boy, who had just arrived from the island of Pico, got a job working for a Portuguese farmer on the outskirts of New Bedford for "five dollars a month, plus room and board."[31] It took him just two weeks to realize that there were more rewarding employment possibilities available and through a friend he was able to get a job in one of New Bedford's cotton mills at $3.50 a week. Out of that $3.50,

he had to pay room and board, but it only came to $2.50 a week and included his laundry. Farming could not compete with industry and, as the boy later recalled, " I went to work, sweeping floors in a cotton mill. In about three months, I was promoted to being a cleaner ..."[32] By 1910, New Bedford had become the center of the manufacturing of fine cotton goods in the United States.[33]

It was in the nearby town of Fall River, the largest textile center in the nation from 1880 until about 1920, that the Portuguese immigrants in New England attained their greatest concentration. The increasing demand for textiles was met by building more and larger mills and employing immigrant men, women, and children to provide the labor. Fall River grew from 74,398 in 1890 to over 100,000 in 1900 when 26,371 individuals, one-quarter of the total population, were employed as textile workers.[34] The Portuguese population of Fall River numbered 104 in 1880, steadily grew to over 500 in 1900, and then suddenly exploded. In 1905, the city had 5,000 Portuguese immigrants; five years later there were more than 10,000.[35] After 1910 Fall River's growth rate started to slow down, but the Portuguese kept coming—in 1920, 22,431 of the city's 120,458 inhabitants were Portuguese and constituted the largest single foreign-born immigrant group with 18.6 percent of the city's total population.[36] In addition to the Portuguese, there were also substantial numbers of Polish, Italian, and Russian immigrants in the city. Many members of the ethnic groups that had traditionally provided the labor for the textile mills during the last part of the 19th century— the English, Irish, and French Canadians—left the Fall River mills during a bitter twenty-six week strike in 1904 and did not return.[37] "The

Portuguese, and to a lesser extent the Poles, became the major source of unskilled operatives after 1900, much as the French Canadians had been in the 1870s. About half of Fall River's entire Portuguese and Polish population was working in the mills by 1910."[38]

In 1900, the 17,885 foreign-born Portuguese in Massachusetts were concentrated in six counties. The major concentration, just as it had been thirty years earlier, was still in Bristol County where 63.5 percent of the Portuguese were located, mostly in either Fall River or New Bedford. Middlesex County accounted for 9.7 percent and most of these were in Lowell, a major textile center. The Portuguese were still important in the fishing industry and 6.9 percent of them lived in Barnstable County, where Provincetown and Cape Cod were located; another 5.6 percent were in Essex County, the home of the fishing port of Gloucester, and the textile town of Lawrence. Suffolk County, which was almost all encompassed by Boston, contained 6.7 percent and the remaining 3.4 percent were in Plymouth County (see Map 3).

By 1910, the Portuguese population of Massachusetts had more than doubled and in 1920, the high point of the second stage of immigration, there were 50,294 foreign-born Portuguese in the state.[39] Between 1920 and 1930 the number of foreign-born Portuguese in Massachusetts declined by 7,000, but the 43,042 Portuguese immigrants living in the state in 1930 were concentrated in the same six counties where they had been thirty years earlier (see Map 3). The only noticeable change was a slightly greater concentration in both Bristol and Middlesex counties, which were already the leading counties in 1900. In spite of low-paying jobs, high infant mortality rates and difficult living conditions, Massachusetts was home to some 62,000 second-generation Portuguese in 1930. Given the nature of the Portuguese community, it is not too surprising that the relative distribution of the 105,076 Portuguese "foreign-stock" in Massachusetts in 1930 was almost identical to the pattern first apparent in the 1900 Census.[40]

Settling in Rhode Island

Rhode Island, like the neighboring state of Massachusetts, was easy to get to from the Azores and had ample employment opportunities to attract the second wave of Portuguese immigrants. It did not, however,

have a substantial Portuguese population in 1870 when only 189 foreign-born Portuguese were counted in the entire state. What it did have
was proximity to Bristol County, Massachusetts, where more than half of
all the Portuguese in Massachusetts were located. Fall River, commonly
referred to as the "border city," abutted Newport County, Rhode Island,
a rural agricultural area, and was only eighteen miles from Providence,
the capital and industrial center of the state. Many Portuguese immigrants "spilled over" into the state from Fall River and New Bedford after
1890 and ended up in nearby Providence where there was a demand for
unskilled laborers. In the early 1900s, Portuguese men in Providence
were employed as "longshoremen and deckhands, coal and brick workers, hand operators in oyster and screw companies, and pork packers in
meat houses."[41] Portuguese women in Rhode Island, like their counterparts in nearby Massachusetts, commonly worked outside the home
mainly in lace factories, laundries and cotton mills.[42]

For many Azoreans toiling as unskilled laborers in the textile mills
of New England, a small farm of their own was a dream to work
toward. For most it remained just that, a dream never quite attained,
and they and their offspring made the permanent transition from rural
folk to urban industrial workers. Others, either more fortunate or more
determined, started out in the mills but were able to save enough
money to get them started in farming. They bought small farms and
took up market gardening and dairying.[43] More typically, for those who
eventually ended up as independent farmers, was the slow progression
from farm laborer, to tenant, to owner of a mortgaged farm, and finally
to the envied position of possessing a clear title to their own farm.[44]
Every change in status was accompanied by deprivation and hard work,
and it was only after they successfully made the transition from farm
laborer to owner that they were occasionally able to indulge in anything
more than the most basic necessities of life.

While Portuguese immigrants in Fall River and New Bedford
worked in the mills and dreamed of owning a farm, many of the farmers in nearby Newport County and elsewhere in New England saw the
new employment possibilities and the increasing amenities of urban
living as a decided improvement over their traditional rural life and
started moving to the cities. They left behind abandoned or idle farms
which they were only too happy to rent and sell to the would-be farm-

ers from the Azores. Portsmouth, Rhode Island, a rural farming community about twelve miles southwest of Fall River, was one of several communities where Portuguese immigrants were successful in getting back to the land. Prior to 1890 there were few Portuguese in Portsmouth. Thirty years later they comprised almost half of the community's population—some 1,177 out of a total population of 2,590. Unlike Fall River, where there were a number of other ethnic groups competing for jobs and housing, the Portuguese constituted virtually the entire foreign element in Portsmouth.[45]

Getting a farm was one thing, making it support a family and pay for itself was something else. Azoreans were not unaccustomed to hard work and niggardly rewards from the soil, but they were forced to employ all the agricultural know-how they had learned in their homeland to make the farmlands of Rhode Island support them.

53

> They are in the fields as long as it is light and employ the labor of every member of their families old enough to wield a hoe. Being in addition exceedingly frugal, and understanding intensive farming, they are successful on New England farms where the native farmer has either failed or found more lucrative employment in the city. Their economic success is often, however, at the expense of the health and happiness of wives and children, and it spells hard work with little recreation for the whole family.[46]

In contrast to life in the nearby mill towns where Portuguese immigrants were surrounded by their countrymen, life for the newcomer to Portsmouth was one of isolation and living conditions were worse in the country than they were in the cities: "Many of the houses are old and poorly equipped and most are, of course, lacking in modern conveniences, but these conditions are the typical rural situation."[47] Economic survival dictated hard work by every member of the family and a willingness to live at a low standard of living and do without many of the things that others in American society considered essentials. They persevered, however, and the number of land-owning versus land-renting Portuguese slowly increased. Portsmouth, for example, witnessed an increase in Portuguese landowners from only one in 1885 to eighty-four in 1920. The determination and industriousness of the

Portuguese soon earned them a reputation as first-class farmers who could make the land produce when no one else could and won the respect of even their most severe critics. As one observer noted, "As a people willing to work in abandoned farms and able to make a living from them, the Portuguese seem to be a real asset."[48] Recognition of their farming ability was epitomized in a saying which became common in New England in the early part of the 20th century: "If you want to see a potato grow, you have to speak to it in Portuguese." As the years passed they were able to make noticeable economic progress, but, as in the mill towns, that progress was achieved through considerable personal sacrifice that entailed long hours of hard work, deprivation from all but the most basic necessities, minimal exposure to education for their children, and little contact with the larger American society.

Whatever their occupation, the Portuguese population of Rhode Island steadily increased after 1890. In 1900, there were 2,545 foreign born Portuguese in the state: 53.7 percent of them resided in Providence County and worked as unskilled labor in the capital city; 32.4 percent lived in rural Newport County; and 10.6 percent in Bristol County (see Map 4). In the next ten years, the Portuguese population increased two-and-a-half times and the Census of 1910 recorded 6,571 foreign-born Portuguese living in Rhode Island.[49] New Portuguese immigrants continued to settle in the state until the restrictive legislation of the mid-1920s effectively curtailed the flow of immigrants to the entire country. The Census of 1930 enumerated 29,097 Portuguese "foreign stock" in Rhode Island; 11,679 were foreign-born and the other 17,418 were their offspring. The major change in the distribution of both foreign-born and second-generation Portuguese in Rhode Island between 1900 and 1930 was an increased urban focus due to the continued attraction of jobs in the Providence area. The growth in the Providence urban area was paralleled by an increase of Portuguese in Bristol County to 20.2 percent and in Kent County, which appears for the first time, with 6.6 percent of the foreign-born in 1930. The more rural area of Newport County continued to experience an absolute increase in its Portuguese population, but its relative percentage statewide declined to 18.3 percent by 1930.

MAP 3

PORTUGUESE POPULATION OF MASSACHUSETTS, 1900

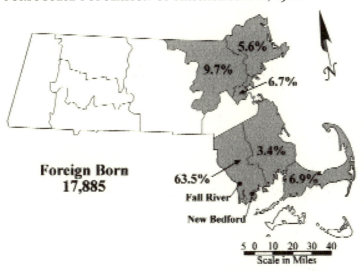

Source:Twelfth Census of the United States, 1900, Vol II, Population, Part 2

PORTUGUESE POPULATION OF MASSACHUSETTS, 1930

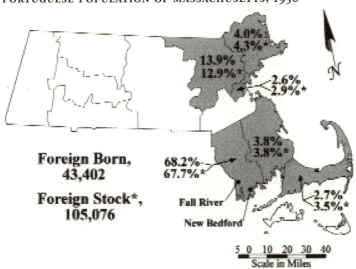

Source:Fifteenth Census of the United States, 1930, Vol III, Population, Part I

Settling in Connecticut

In many ways Connecticut was similar to Rhode Island: it was as close as either Massachusetts or Rhode Island to the Azores, although not quite so accessible; there were jobs for unskilled laborers in the state's developing industries; and, it had a small (221) foreign-born Portuguese population in 1870. The similarities ended there. Most importantly, it did not share Rhode Island's proximity to a large Portuguese immigrant population. New London, known as the Whaling City in Connecticut, was comparable to New Bedford in that most of the Portuguese in Connecticut in 1870 were there as a result of whaling. Between 1870 and 1900 most of the Portuguese immigrants who went to Connecticut joined friends or re-latives already living there. In 1900, then, the major concentration of Portuguese in Connecticut was in New London County, where the former whaling port of New London was located. Although eighty-eight percent of the Portuguese in Connecticut were in New London County, there were only 568 foreign-born Portuguese in the entire state. Five percent of those were in Hartford County, the major industrial center of the state, and another four percent were in New Haven County, which was the location of both the port of New Haven and the industrial city of Meriden.

Virtually all of the increase in Portuguese immigration into Connecticut between 1900 and 1930 was to the industrial centers of the state. The foreign-born population reached 2,345 and the "foreign stock," a category that included immigrants and their American-born children, reached 4,701 in 1930. The total Portuguese population of New London County increased only slightly while the county's percentage of the state total dropped from 88.2 percent in 1900 to 24.7 percent in 1930. Other noticeable changes were in Fairfield County, which accounted for 25.9 percent of the state's foreign-born Portuguese population in 1930 and New Haven and Hartford Counties, which increased to 26.1 percent and 18.7 percent respectively (see Map 4).

Working and Living Conditions

The demand for textiles and the abundant supply of cheap immigrant labor that kept the mills running created a boom economy in Fall River

MAP 4

PORTUGUESE POPULATION OF CONNECTICUT & RHODE ISLAND, 1900

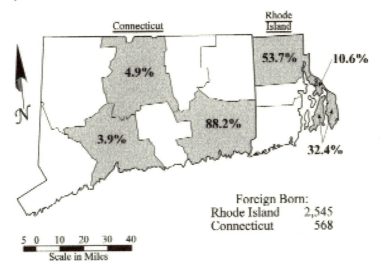

Foreign Born:
Rhode Island   2,545
Connecticut   568

Source: Twelfth Census of the United States, 1900, Vol. II, Population, Part 2.

PORTUGUESE POPULATION OF CONNECTICUT & RHODE ISLAND, 1930

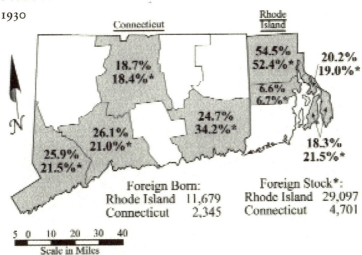

Foreign Born:
Rhode Island   11,679
Connecticut   2,345

Foreign Stock*:
Rhode Island   29,097
Connecticut   4,701

Source: Fifteenth Census of the United States, 1930,
Vol. III, Population, Parts 1 & 2.

and other mill towns in Massachusetts and Rhode Island. The benefits, however, did not extend to all members of the society. The immigrant populations were massed at the bottom of the social and economic ladder and suffered grievously from low wages, poor working conditions, overcrowded housing and inadequate health and social services. Unskilled and uneducated, the Portuguese filled the lower-paying occupational categories in the mills. Economic necessity motivated most of the able-bodied members of a family to seek employment in the mills where women and children, as well as men, became industrial workers. As one observer noted, "If they marry, they must either live on a very low plane or expect their wives and children to continue to work outside the home... "[50]Working outside the home was not new to Portuguese women and children as it had been a part of life in the subsistence-agrarian economy of their homeland. Working conditions were quite different in the cotton mills from what they had been in the fields, however, and the differences soon began to show themselves, albeit, in a subtle and devious fashion.

By 1910, the Portuguese in Fall River and New Bedford were attracting attention by their excessive infant mortality rates, which were among the highest in the nation. In both communities the Portuguese suffered infant mortality rates in excess of 200 per 1,000 births—more than double the national average.[51] The continued high infant mortality rates for Portuguese mothers prompted a number of studies which attempted to isolate the major factors responsible for the elevated number of infant deaths.[52] A perceptive Fall River doctor concluded that:

The foreign-born mother in Fall River, for example, is more likely to work in the mills during pregnancy, to have many children, and to live in crowded and unhygienic quarters. She, more than the native mother, reflects the injurious influences of an unfavorable industrial and economic climate.[53]

Subsequent studies revealed that Portuguese mothers in Fall River were employed to a larger degree than mothers of any other nationality and that thirty-nine percent of the Portuguese mothers were employed outside their household during pregnancy, more than double the rate for other expectant mothers in the community.[54]

The Portuguese of Fall River in 1920, some 22,431 individuals, constituted a young, expanding population in need of housing and living space. Forty-five percent of the Portuguese community had been born in the United States and thirty percent were nine years old or younger. Children fourteen years old and younger made up forty-one percent of the population, while only eleven percent of the total population was more than forty-five years old.[55] The large numbers of poorly-paid immigrants were hard-pressed to find adequate housing in Fall River and usually ended up with their families crowded into tenement houses:

> The sections of the city where most of the Portuguese live are unattractive. There is a dreary monotony of plain two and three story frame buildings with accommodations for from two to twelve families, sometimes fronting the street, and sometimes ugly alleys. In most yards the tramp of many feet has prevented the growth of grass although there are exceptions to this. Even where the interiors of the tenements are well kept, hallways are apt to be defaced and uncleanly.[56]

59

In the face of economic adversity, the forces which sustained the Portuguese immigrants in the mill towns of New England were the same forces which had sustained them in their homeland: their family, religion, and community. They came to the United States in search of economic opportunity and that meant that every able-bodied member of the family had to take jobs in a factory. Uneducated themselves, for the most part Portuguese parents saw little need for their children to receive an education. While schools were a convenient place to send the young children, particularly if the mother had to work, for the older children it merely delayed their entry into a paying occupation which would assist the family. Most of the children of immigrant parents left school as soon as the law permitted and sought employment.[57]

Identity, Culture, and Community

Outside the family, the Portuguese community maintained its identity through the continued use of their native language and their strong affiliation with the Catholic Church. By 1920, Fall River supported six Catholic Churches and fourteen priests.[58] Religion, their solace in times of sorrow, was also the focal point of the happy occasions in their lives. The dreariness and drudgery of everyday life were offset by the joys of birth and community participation in the sacraments of the Church. Baptisms, confirmations, and weddings were all occasions for celebration and festivities. When they came to the United States, the Azoreans also brought with them their tradition of celebrating certain religious holidays. Although these celebrations or *festas* reflected their religious heritage, much of the activity was secular in nature and took place outside the Church itself. The celebration of the Feast of the Holy Ghost, the major celebration in Azorean communities, usually lasted for several days and provided ample opportunities to dance the *chamarrita* and other traditional dances, listen to the singing contests between extemporaneous composers, renew old acquaintances, and strengthen family ties. The *festa* concluded on Sunday with a procession through the streets of the city. Led by a band, the procession included groups of men carrying the statues of saints from the church, followed by members of the various religious fraternities. The parade terminated at the church where a High Mass was conducted in Portuguese for the participants and other members of the community. The *festa* concluded with the serving of a traditional meal of meat and bread to the entire community.

60

The vernacula was not introduced until 1965 ? Mass would have been in Latin

The Blessing of the Fleet in Gloucester and Provincetown, the Feast of the Blessed Sacrament in New Bedford, and the Feast of the Holy Ghost in New Bedford and Fall River were special occasions in the Portuguese communities of New England and were always well attended. Children born in this country were immersed in a Portuguese-speaking culture and learned the traditions of their parents' homeland. Adults reaffirmed their ties to the Portuguese community and maintained contact with members of their extended family. The religious celebrations were also instrumental in maintaining the social networks that existed within the Portuguese communities in the United States and between the United States and the Azores. The latest information about friends and conditions in the islands, about new job opportunities, and about the availability of housing circulated rapidly at the *festas*. The *festas* were an important part of the Portuguese community and helped maintain its viability as a recognizable ethnic group—in an area crowded with ethnics. In addition, the celebrations provided a temporary escape from the monotony of day-to-day living.

The Portuguese community lived together, worshipped together and celebrated together. Although this close relationship was instrumental in maintaining the cohesiveness of the community, it effectively delayed the normal acculturation process. Many Portuguese immigrants were slow to learn English and other aspects of American culture that could have facilitated upward mobility. A young boy living in New Bedford at the time later recalled, "I had no opportunity to learn any English. I worked with Portuguese people and lived with Portuguese people all during that time. Even my boss was Portuguese."[59]

New arrivals joined relatives or friends already living in the city or stayed in lodging houses with other Portuguese-speaking immigrants. They depended heavily upon informal contacts with friends and relatives to secure employment. "Because most jobs came through unofficial middlemen, the type and place of employment usually followed residential and family patterns."[60] The existence of a strong social network, which played such an important role in obtaining employment and housing, was instrumental in reinforcing local community ties and discouraging integration with non-Portuguese in the community. Within their tight-knit community, which consisted primarily of Azoreans from the islands of São Miguel and Faial, they shared the social customs common to their homeland and maintained a very high degree of intermarriage. It was not uncommon for marriage partners to be from the same hometown in the Azores.[61] New immigrants relied almost exclusively upon "their fellow Portuguese for advice, money, and ethnic support because of their tendencies to group together and to shun public charity."[62]

Unable to capitalize on the economic advantages of education, the immigrants and their children had little chance for advancement in the mills. To improve their economic status, several members of the family had to work; even then their meager resources had to be frugally managed. In many ways, their situation in the United States was not too different from what it had been in the islands, except that here there were many opportunities for employment. Those opportunities for employment continued to attract Portuguese immigrants until they were excluded by restrictive legislation in 1921 and 1924.

Return and Restriction

In the absence of any restrictive legislation, the total number of immigrants undoubtedly would have continued to increase during the 1920s. However, a growing nativist movement developed in the United States in the 1880s, fueled by labor unrest in the industrial centers and a growing concern that America was becoming overcrowded and changing too rapidly. "The beginning of significant southern and eastern European immigration, and the onset of economic depression in 1893, made the danger seem more acute.[63] Many perceived these new immigrants as "inferior, peculiarly unfitted to contribute to American society"[64] and, in fact, as a threat to their vision of the traditional American society. Agitation to curtail, or at least restrict, this tide of "undesirable" immigrants increased and finally resulted in the establishment of a literacy requirement for all immigrants in 1917. By overwhelming majorities, the Congress decided to require immigrants over sixteen to read a short passage in a language of their choice.[65] Illiteracy thereby became the first means of substantially reducing the flow of immigration.

The literacy requirement was exceptionally onerous for the Portuguese immigrants who came from a rural, nonindustrial, agrarian society that offered little opportunity for its members to acquire even a rudimentary education. The rate of illiteracy among Portuguese immigrants over fourteen who entered the United States between 1899 and 1917 ranged from a high in 1907 of 76.5 percent to a low in 1915 of 54.2 percent.[66] The impact of the new legislation was immediate and severe. In 1916, 12,208 Portuguese immigrants were admitted to the United States, by 1918 the number of immigrants had declined to 2,319, and the following year only 1,574 were allowed in.[67]

The rapid rise in the number of Portuguese immigrants arriving after 1900 was accompanied by a steady increase in emigrants leaving the United States to return home. It was common practice for young men who had emigrated to America to work until they could save enough money to return to the Azores and take a wife. Many returned immediately with their new bride. Others remained in the islands hoping to use their accumulated capital to become successful farmers or merchants. Some were successful while others watched their money dwindle away and reluctantly decided to return to the United States, this time accompanied

[handwritten margin note: and by a belief in eugenics]

by a wife and children. Still others returned to marry a wife only to find that she refused to leave her family and were themselves forced to remain in the islands. Such was the case with one man who left the islands in his youth as a crewman on a whaler and had worked in the Central Valley of California for eighteen years. Finally able to realize his dream of returning to his homeland to marry and raise a family, he found that the land of his youth had changed. Unable to persuade his wife to leave the islands, he spent the remainder of his life there. His children, however, followed their father's earlier example and eventually emigrated to California.[68]

There were also those who returned to the Azores with the intention of staying and, finding that they could no longer adjust to the slow pace of village life, soon departed again.[69] Others found life in the United States lacking many of the traditional values they had acquired as Azoreans and decided that they preferred the lifestyle of their homeland to that of America. In the twelve years between 1908 and 1919, no less than 20,751 Portuguese returned to the Azores from the United States.[70] Return migration fluctuated with conditions in the United States, and ranged from a low of 816 in 1909 to a high of 3,525 in 1919. Of those returning from the United States between 1909 and 1919, 68.9 percent had been in the U.S. five years or less, 24.9 percent between five and ten years, 4.1 percent from ten to fifteen, and only 2.1 percent for more than fifteen years.[71]

63

Undoubtedly, the war raging in Europe had some influence on the decline of Azorean immigration. The war fueled the nativist movement in the United States that was demanding still more restrictive immigration legislation. In 1921, the Three Percent Law was enacted, which established a quota for the number of immigrants admitted from a particular country at three percent of the residents from that country living in the United States in 1910. The Portuguese annual quota, based on that formula, was substantially reduced to 2,520.[72] The Three Percent Law was followed by more restrictive legislation in 1924. The end result of the new legislation was "to cut the total immigration, to ensure that European immigration did not much exceed that from the Americas, and to impose drastic cuts in the movement from southern and eastern Europe."[73] America was no longer the "free port" for immigrants the world over.

Notes

[1] Alexander Starbuck, *History of the American Whale Fishery from Its Earliest Inception to the Year 1876* (New York, 1964), 1-20. In the last half of the 20th century "whaling" was transformed into a dirty word in the United States—an unlawful and despicable occupation that many would like to see banned worldwide. Such, however, was not always the case in this country. The occasional killing of whales that swam along the coastline was already a well-established practice among the indigenous population when the first European colonist arrived to settle in the New England colonies. The new arrivals were quick to follow the example of the natives and, in some cases, even copied their hunting techniques. Throughout the 17th century, shore whaling was sporadically carried on along the seaboard of the New York and New England colonies. Shore whalers lived along the coast and towed the captured whales to shore for processing. The success of the various shore whaling companies was primarily dependent upon the number of whales that chanced to swim close enough to shore to be observed and then pursued.

Early in the 18th century, ships were outfitted for short voyages to search for whales away from the shoreline. Two desirable characteristics of the sperm whale became apparent about this time making this species the preferred target of these whalers. Sperm whales have a large closed cavity in their head which contains a mixture of spermaceti, a waxy solid used in making ointments and candles, and oil—the finest oil from whales. In addition to being sought for the superior quality of their oil, the bodies of dead sperm whales float and are thus less likely to be lost after they are killed than are the carcasses of other species of whales. On these early cruises, which lasted up to six weeks, the blubber was removed from the whale and stored in barrels aboard ship until the vessel returned to shore where the trying-out took place. The size of whaling ships gradually increased, but the continued necessity of returning to port to render the voluminous blubber into oil served as the ultimate constraint to sailing range and time at sea. This restriction eventually prompted a major technological innovation among the whalers—the construction of a special area where the try pots could be housed on board and the trying-out completed at sea. Ship records indicate that some vessels were equipped with try works as early as 1762 (Starbuck). With the last major constraint lifted, whaling vessels sailed widely over the Atlantic Ocean in pursuit of their quarry during the last third of the 18th century— from the North Atlantic in the summer to the South Atlantic in winter (Charles Scammon, *The Marine Mammals of the North-Western Coast of North America* [San Francisco, 1874], 209).

[2] In 1775, on the eve of the American Revolution, 304 vessels with a total of 4,059 seamen were employed in whaling—and most of those were out of Massachusetts. The losses suffered by the whalers and whaling ports were substantial during the Revolutionary War, as they were later during the War of 1812 and the Civil War of the 1860s, but each time the industry rebounded after the cessation of hostilities.

[3] The lay system minimized the ship's expenses and motivated the crew to spot and kill every whale possible. When a ship returned from a cruise, the whale products were sold at the going rate and the expenses incurred in outfitting the ship were deducted, as were the owners' share of the profits. The remainder was divided among the crew based on their relative importance to the whaling operation as indicated by the pay they agreed to when they signed on the voyage—the captain and officers of the crew received the largest shares and the common sailors the smallest. Any supplies that a crewman needed while at sea were provided from the ship's stores and charged against the individual's share.

[4] Collectively known as the Azores, the chain actually consists of three groups of islands: Santa Maria and São Miguel—the most easterly pair; Terceira, Graciosa, São Jorge, Pico and Faial—the central group; and Corvo and Flores—situated on the northwest periphery of the archipelago.

[5] Herman Melville, *Moby Dick or The Whale* (New York, 1950 [1851]), 118.

[6] Walter Frederick Walker, *The Azores or Western Islands: A Political, Commercial and Geographical Account* (London, 1886), 279.

[7] Josef Berger, *In Great Waters: The Story of the Portuguese Fishermen* (New York, 1941), 45-46.

[8] Robert Clarke, "Open Boat Whaling in the Azores," *Discovery Reports* 26: 352.

[9] An individual's personal network consists of the chains of persons with whom that individual is in actual contact, and their interconnections. A social network is the composite of individual communication networks within a given society. For a discussion of social networks see Jeremy Boissevain, *Friends of Friends: Networks, Manipulators and Coalitions* (Oxford, 1974), 24-78.

[10] In that particular census (*Ninth Census of the United States, 1870*. Vol. 1.), Portuguese included those individuals from the Atlantic Islands (the Azores, Madeira and Cape Verde Islands) and mainland Portugal. The census also distinguished between white and colored; of the 8,971 Portuguese, 257 were classified as colored and were, no doubt, former whalers from the Cape Verde Islands—a small group of black-inhabited islands off the west coast of Africa that belonged to Portugal. Another 109 of the total were living in territories belonging to the United States.

One-tenth of the total Portuguese population of the United States in 1870 was accounted for by a group of 856 Madeira Islanders who had been driven out of their homeland because they had converted to the Presbyterian religion; the Presbyterian Church in the United States subsequently went to their aid and helped resettle them in Illinois. See Sandra Wolforth, *The Portuguese in America* (San Francisco, 1978), 10.

[11] Donald R. Taft, *Two Portuguese Communities in New England* (New York, 1923), 97.

[12] *Ninth Census of the United States, 1870*. Vol. 1.

[13] Samuel Eliot Morison, *The Maritime History of Massachusetts 1783-1860* (New York, 1921), 231-32. "A packetline meant two or more vessels whose owners advertised sailing to designated ports, on schedules as regular as wind and weather permitted; and which depended for their profit on freight and passengers furnished by the public rather than goods shipped on the owner's account."

[14] Zeph W. Pease and George A. Hough, *New Bedford, Massachusetts: Its History, Institutions and Attractions* (New Bedford, 1889), 65.

[15] Lawrence Oliver, *Never Backward: The Autobiography of Lawrence Oliver—A Portuguese-American* (San Diego, 1972), 13.

[16] Taft, *Two Portuguese Communities*, 101.

[17] Ibid., 95.

[18] Ibid., 102.

[19] Ibid., 101.

[20] Morison, *The Maritime History of Massachusetts 1783-1860*, 316.

[21] Pease and Hough, *New Bedford, Massachusetts*, 31.

[22] Morison, *The Maritime History of Massachusetts 1783-1860*, 375.

[23] Berger, *In Great Waters*, 53-61.

[24] Morison, *The Maritime History of Massachusetts 1783-1860*, 352.

[25] *Leading Manufacturers and Merchants of Eastern Massachusetts: Historical and Descriptive Review of the Industrial Enterprises of Bristol, Plymouth, Norfolk and Middlesex Counties* (New York, 188?), 30-36.

[26] Pease and Hough, *New Bedford, Massachusetts*, 149-153.

[27] Berger, *In Great Waters*, 58.

[28] Ibid., 79

[29] Taft, *Two Portuguese Communities*, 134.

[30] Pease and Hough, *New Bedford, Massachusetts*, 153.

65

[31] Oliver, *Never Backward*, 15.

[32] Ibid., 17.

[33] Seymour Luis Wolfbein, *The Decline of a Cotton Textile City: A Study of New Bedford* (New York, 1944), 10.

[34] Philip T. Silva, Jr., "The Position of 'New' Immigrants in the Fall River Textile Industry," *International Migration Review,* 10, no. 2 (1976): 221.

[35] Ibid., 224-25.

[36] Taft, *Two Portuguese Communities,* 199.

[37] Silva, "The Position of 'New' Immigrants in the Fall River Textile Industry," 222-23.

[38] Ibid., 225-26.

[39] *Fourteenth Census of the United States, 1920,* Vol. 3 (Washington, D.C., 1920).

[40] In addition to the foreign-born population, the Census of 1930 included a category labeled "white foreign stock" which included immigrants and their children.

[41] Susan T. Ferst, "The Immigration and the Settlement of the Portuguese in Providence: 1890 to 1924." (MA Thesis, Brown University, 1972), 22.

[42] Ibid., 23.

[43] Leo Pap, *Portuguese American Speech: An Outline of Speech Conditions Among the Portuguese Immigrants in New England and Elsewhere in the United States* (New York, 1949), 13.

[44] Taft, *Two Portuguese Communities,* 258.

[45] Ibid., 196-202.

[46] Ibid., 255.

[47] Ibid., 228.

[48] Ibid., 349.

[49] *Thirteenth Census of the United States, 1910,* Vol. 2 (Washington, DC, 1910).

[50] Taft, *Two Portuguese Communities,* 247.

[51] Ibid., 166.

[52] Among the variables considered were: ethnicity, level of education, ability to speak English, living conditions, length of residence in the United States, whether or not the mother breast-fed her baby, and income level.

[53] Taft, *Two Portuguese Communities,* 164.

[54] Ibid., 164-77.

[55] Ibid., 199-200.

[56] Ibid., 225.

[57] Ibid., 308.

[58] Ibid., 338.

[59] Oliver, *Never Backward,* 18.

[60] Ferst, "The Immigration and the Settlement of the Portuguese in Providence: 1890 to 1924," 25.

[61] Ibid., 25-32.

[62] Ibid., 32.

[63] P. Taylor, *The Distant Magnet: European Emigration to the USA* (New York, 1971), 243.

[64] Ibid., 243.

[65] Ibid., 247.

[66] Taft, *Two Portuguese Communities,* 116.

[67] Ibid., 101.

[68] An interview with Alexandrina Alves in Patterson, California on November 25, 1978. Her father lived in the United States eighteen years before he returned to the Azores and married her mother.

[69] Borges de Henriques, *A Trip to the Azores or Western Islands* (Boston, 1867), 104.

[70] Taft, *Two Portuguese Communities*, 101.
[71] Ibid., 117.
[72] Ibid., 102.
[73] Taylor, *The Distant Magnet*, 255.

CHAPTER III

LIFE IN THE WEST

California

There was considerable contact between California and New England prior to 1849 and many a sailor successfully jumped ship in San Francisco to escape intolerable conditions on board. But in the early part of the 19th century, California could not have been an overly attractive place to stay. Settlements were small, few and far between. Isolated as they were from Mexico, the occupants were forced to be self-sufficient in almost everything and the local economy provided little, other than cowhides, to exchange with the occasional merchant ship. The first record of a permanent Portuguese resident was that of António José Rocha, who, along with nine other men, deserted an English ship in Monterey in 1815. Foreigners were not welcome in California at that time and the other deserters were returned to their ship. Rocha, skilled as a carpenter and blacksmith, was also a Catholic of Latin heritage and, for whatever reasons, not returned to his ship. He eventually made his way to the Los Angeles area, married and settled there.[2] One deserter, however, hardly constitutes a migration, and the total number of foreigners living in California increased very slowly. By 1830, about 150 foreigners were living in the area and only five of those were Portuguese.[3]

In 1850, the Nantucket and New Bedford fleets were whaling in the Arctic waters of the Pacific Ocean, an 18,000 mile voyage down the east coast of South America, around Cape Horn and up the West Coast to the bowhead whaling grounds on the north shores of Alaska.[4] San Francisco was a regular port of call for these ships and provided a final opportunity to replenish supplies before completing the journey to the Alaskan whaling grounds. Stopping to replenish supplies also provided

Rural Portuguese Family in California, 1904.

California Dairy Farm, 1910.

Hawaiian Sugar Plantation with Sugar Mill and Houses
for Workers, circa 1915.

Portuguese Family on the Island of Hawaii, 1904.

an opportunity for disenchanted sailors to desert ship. Desertion was always a potential problem for captains of whaling ships. After the discovery of gold in 1849, however, desertions reached epidemic proportions as the stories of gold waiting to be picked up and fortunes easily made tempted many sailors to strike out for the gold fields. One historian noted that "after the discovery of the gold mines in California, desertions from the ships were numerous and often causeless, generally in such numbers as to seriously cripple the efficiency of the ships."[5] Azoreans, and many others, availed themselves of this cheap and illegal passage to California as whaleships brought both the news of the gold strike in California and the means to get there.[6] San Francisco Bay and the Sacramento River were the last port that many whaling ships ever made and, without a doubt, the discovery of gold in California contributed to the eventual demise of whaling in the United States. Many whaling vessels began avoiding San Francisco in an attempt to hold on to their crews and the Hawaiian Islands, where some Azorean sailors also chose to jump ship, became a center for refitting and supplying the Pacific whaling fleet.

In spite of the desertions in California, the Azoreans acquired a reputation as hard-working, dependable whalers, and the practice of sailing from New England to the Azores, with a skeleton crew that would be filled out with islanders, became commonplace in the 1850s. The aura of the gold fields and the general attraction of California continued to draw Azoreans from their island home to America and during this period the majority of the newcomers ended up on the West Coast instead of the East. Between 1860 and 1870, the number of Portuguese in California doubled and reached a new high of 3,435—forty percent of the Portuguese population in the United States.

Gold Fever

When word of the California gold strike reached New England in 1849, many sea captains were already experienced in sailing around Cape Horn and up the West Coast of North America. The rush was on! The first outpouring from the East Coast consisted of men anxious to be first in the gold fields. As one observer noted, "The gold fever drained Nantucket of one-quarter of its voting population in nine months. In the same period, 800 men left New Bedford for the mines."[7] Some of these first gold-seekers were Portuguese sailing from New Bedford and Nantucket, either as passengers or crew. The initial rush to find gold was followed by a determined effort on the part of those who had remained at home to share in this newfound wealth. There was an immediate need for all kinds of food and merchandise to outfit these argonauts departing daily from San Francisco and Sacramento. The merchants of New England were quick to respond. Again ships and sailors were needed to get the cargo to California quickly and for many, it was a one-way trip. "In July 1850," for example, the lure of gold left "512 abandoned vessels lying in front of the city of San Francisco, some with unloaded cargoes."[8] Most of the Portuguese who availed themselves of the slow-moving whalers missed the frenzied rush to be first, but there was still gold to be found when they arrived. As they soon learned, though, finding gold was not an easy task.

79

The geography of California was not well known in the 1840s and what many hopeful prospectors expected would be a relatively quick trip to pick up gold nuggets lying on the ground turned out quite differently. Instead, they discovered that it was a long journey in 1849 from San Francisco to the Mother Lode, by boat, horse or afoot, and even longer to the Klamath Mountains at the north end of the Sacramento Valley. The would-be miner without sufficient resources to purchase the necessary equipment and supplies to sustain him in his search had little chance of success and many of the new arrivals were acutely short of capital. As it turned out, getting to the gold fields was the easiest part of being a gold miner. Once there, the real problems presented themselves. Food was difficult to obtain and when it was available it was frequently poor in quality and always exorbitantly priced; living conditions were miserable and many miners had only rudimentary shelters that offered little protection from the harsh winter weather in the Sierra Nevada Mountains; little, if any, medical treatment was available and there was little hope for the unfortunate miner who became seriously ill or injured; and there was the constant threat of claim jumpers or robbers. Many '49ers became discouraged after a year or two and departed from the gold fields. Those that were financially able frequently returned home; the rest sought a way to earn a living in California.

How many Portuguese were in California in 1850 and whether or not they were engaged in mining is not precisely known. The first official census of California was taken in 1850 under, admittedly, adverse conditions. The population was migratory and transient and the result was, at best, a rough estimate. One hundred and nine Portuguese were enumerated in that census out of a total population of 92,597.⁹ The Portuguese first began to arrive in California, in any appreciable numbers, in the 1850s. By 1860, when the next official census was conducted, the state's population had increased to 379,994 and 1,580 were listed as born in either Portugal or the Atlantic Islands.¹⁰ No doubt most of them were attracted to California by the gold rush: the census for that year reveals that there were 844 Portuguese miners scattered around the gold fields of California. The majority went to the Mother Lode country east of Sacramento, but a group of them wound up in the extreme northern part of the state in Hawkinsville, "the only Portuguese-dominated mining settlement [that] persisted throughout the latter part of the nineteenth century."¹¹ As late as 1880, Hawkinsville, never much more than a collection of miners' shacks, still had 313 inhabitants and 175 of them were Portuguese.

The early, labor-intensive days of placer mining, where alluvial deposits were panned to find particles of gold washed down from higher elevations, gradually gave way to more capital-intensive, hard-rock mining which involved following a vein of gold-bearing quartz into the side of a mountain by sinking shafts or blasting tunnels. The resulting ore had to be crushed in a stamp mill to separate the gold from the quartz and bedrock. Mining companies were better able to support the costs involved in both hard-rock and hydraulic mining, where entire hillsides were washed away with high-pressure streams of water. For the individual miner, the choice increasingly came down to working for a large mining corporation for wages or getting out of mining. Many took the latter alternative.

Whaling and Fishing

In many ways the life of a gold miner was not unlike that of a whaler: the hours were long, the work was hard and the rewards uncertain. Disappointed miners began abandoning the mining fields in the early

MAP 5

SHORE WHALING STATIONS, CALIFORNIA, 1854-1880

Crescent City

Bolinas Bay
Halfmoon Bay
Pigeon Point
Santa Cruz
Monterey Bay (2)
Carmel Bay
Point Sur

San Simeon

Port Horford

Cojo Viejo · Goleta

Portuguese Bend · Dead Man's Island

San Diego Bay (2)

Scale of Kilometers
0 25 50   100   200

Scale of Miles
0   25   50   100   200

1850s and turning to other occupations. The natural inclination was to employ whatever skills and experiences an individual already possessed. A number of Portuguese turned back to the sea. As early as 1854, some of these former whalers decided to try their luck in California waters. In 1854, a San Francisco newspaper reported, "A number of Portuguese fishermen have caught twenty-four whales of all kinds in the bay of Monterey since April last."[12] During the next thirty years, Portuguese whalers from the Azores established shore whaling stations at a number of points along the California coast from Crescent City, near the Oregon border, to San Diego (see Map 5). Many of these whaling stations resembled coastal villages in the Azores:

> Scattered around the foothills, which come to the water's edge, are the nearby whitewashed cabins of the whalers, nearly all of whom are Portuguese, from the Azores or Western Islands of the Atlantic. They have their families with them, and keep a pig, sheep, goat, or cow, prowling around the premises; these, with a small garden-patch, yielding principally corn and pumpkins, make up the general picture of the hamlet...[13]

These whalers pursued the gray whales that annually migrate from the Arctic waters around Alaska to the mating and calving grounds off Baja California in the winter and then back again in the spring. Their habit of migrating along the coastline made them an easy target for exploitation by shore whalers. The life of a whaling station depended upon how successful the men were; some were very short-lived while others were in more or less continuous operation until shore-whaling was finally abandoned in the 1880s. Some stations were well organized commercial operations, others consisted of a few fishermen who would get together and decide to try their luck at whaling during the slack fishing seasons, or men who were farmers part of the year and whalers in the winter and spring.[14] Almost all of the shore-whalers, however, were Azoreans and occasionally the same men were involved in shore-whaling at several different locations. A typical example was,

> Captain Frank Anderson, who is now said to be the most experienced whaling captain on the coast, is a native of the Azores, his Portuguese name having been dropped on naturalization in the United States, as is

the general custom among the natives of the Azores. He was first a
whaler on ships from New Bedford, then came to California in 1866,
and since 1873 he has had charge of whaling camps as captain. He was
at San Luis Obispo until 1874, at Portuguese Bend till 1877, and at
Pigeon Point until 1879, when he with his entire company moved to
Cojo Viejo.[15]

The combination of over-exploitation of the whale population, difficulty in securing seamen, and increased competition from petroleum
products gradually changed the image of the whaling industry, after
about 1870, from a very profitable enterprise to a very risky one.
Although whaling disappeared as an economic activity by the turn of
the century, a relatively small number of Portuguese in California continued to earn their livelihood as commercial fishermen. The San
Francisco Bay Area was the early center of Portuguese fishing, but in
1876 a small group of Azoreans, who had been working as fishermen
in Gloucester, Massachusetts, decided to move to California. Part of
the group went to the San Francisco area and the others ended up in
the small city of San Diego, where they settled on a point of land across
the bay from the main part of town. Point Loma, as the area was
named, gradually evolved into a self-sufficient Portuguese fishing community reminiscent of the Azores. The families raised their own fruit
and vegetables, carried wood from the hills and beaches for cooking,
and even brought fresh water in barrels from across the bay.[16] The
Portuguese and Italians dominated the fresh fish business in San Diego;
what was not sold locally was dried and sent north to the Central
Valley. In the early part of the 20th century, they began to pack the fish
in ice and ship them to Los Angeles. As the fresh fish business pros-
pered, the immigrant fishermen maintained the tradition of encouraging relatives and friends to join them.

The impetus for a major change in the Portuguese community of
San Diego came out of World War I and the efforts to preserve fish by
canning. In 1919, a Portuguese fisherman was hired to supply a local
cannery with fresh tuna and the first attempt was made to preserve that
particular variety of fish in a can.[17] Such was the beginning of the commercial tuna fishing fleet of San Diego and the Portuguese association
with that industry. The San Diego tuna fleet grew rapidly after 1920

83

and was manned predominantly by Portuguese fishermen.[18] Although
the number of Portuguese involved in the catching and canning of tuna
remained small in relation to the total Portuguese population of
California, they played a major role in the development of the tuna
industry in San Diego. As the tuna fleet grew so did the close-knit
Portuguese community on Point Loma and the association between the
two was sufficiently strong that many of the people in San Diego came
to refer to Point Loma as "Tunaville."[19] The technology employed in
tuna fishing has changed radically since those early days in 1920, but
the Portuguese have retained a prominent place in the industry.

84   ## Agriculture

Another occupation one-time whalers and disappointed miners turned
to by the 1870s was commercial agriculture. In contrast to the East
Coast of the United States, most of the land suitable for cultivation in
California was settled in the last half of the 19th century. For the individual with a knowledge of farming and the inclination to use it, the
possibilities seemed unlimited. Although most of the land suitable for
agriculture was already privately owned, it was not being farmed intensively. Much of the land in California was being utilized to graze cattle,
an extensive system of land use, but the large landholdings needed to
support a family in such a system were unnecessary and, in fact, waste-
ful in the eyes of the Portuguese and other immigrants who were accustomed to making do with less. Being able to make the land produce
was a necessity instilled in Azoreans from early childhood; to survive in
their homeland they had to learn how to maximize production from
every bit of land. It was only natural that Portuguese immigrants
applied that same knowledge and determination to farming in
California. As an observer noted,

> It hurts a Portuguese to waste an inch of land. He'll buy the best land out
> of doors— knows the best when he sees it too—and will pay a top price
> without question or flinching; but after he gets it he wants every inch of
> it to be working for him, night and day, every minute of the growing sea-
> son. One of these town orchards in San Leandro has currants between
> the orchard rows, beans between the currant rows, a row of beans close

on each side of the trees, and beans from the end of the rows to the wheeltracks in the street. Not satisfied with this degree of intensiveness and interplanting, the owner doubled the number of rows in the space or corner where his private sidewalk joined the public street.[20]

Confident that they could earn a living on a relatively small piece of land and encouraged by the success of their countrymen who had taken up farming when most other newcomers were still searching for gold, Portuguese immigrants increasingly turned to agriculture for a livelihood. Converting the dream of being an independent farmer into reality, however, was seldom an easy task. Almost all of the Portuguese arrived in California with little or no money. In its place, they brought a willingness to work and endure hardships and personal sacrifice to achieve their goals. Most of those who ended up as independent farmers slowly progressed from working for wages to tenant farming and eventually to private ownership of the land they tilled. The process usually took years.[21]

85

The areas around San Francisco Bay, the arrival and departure point for the passengers and cargo bound for California, and Sacramento, the entrepot to the gold fields, were rapidly settled by people seeking an alternative to an uncertain life searching for gold. In the Census of 1860, one in every four Portuguese man listed his occupation as some type of agricultural activity. Alameda and Contra Costa, the two counties directly across the Bay from San Francisco, had the greatest concentration of Portuguese, followed by the area around Sacramento in Yolo and Sacramento counties.[22] Utilizing the intensive farming techniques of their homeland, the Portuguese farmers raised fruit and vegetables that found a ready market in the nearby cities.

In the early 1870s, the Portuguese in Alameda County, directly across the Bay from San Francisco, were noted as being "amongst the most thriving portion of our population, occupying as they do, small farms of the best land and growing vegetables and fruit."[23] With the largest concentration of people in the state at that time, the San Francisco Bay Area provided a ready market for the agricultural produce of the region. Proximity to this market increased the value of Bay Area land, but the Portuguese, certain that good agricultural land would pay for itself, were willing to pay high prices for small parcels. In fact, a writer in Alameda

County was prompted to note, with tongue in cheek, "A Portuguese advancing toward your premises for the purpose of negotiating a purchase, adds much greater enhancement to its value than the assurances of having a railroad pass through your veranda."[24]

As new immigrants continued to buy land in and around San Leandro, a farming community in Alameda County, it gradually became known as the Portuguese center in the Bay Area. In contrast to the size of traditional California landholdings, most Portuguese farms were quite small. In 1908, the United States Immigration Commission interviewed Portuguese farmers in San Leandro as part of their *Immigrant Farmers in the Western States* study and found the average Portuguese farm holding was 46.6 acres while the median farm size was 12.5 acres.[25] Like many other farmers in the United States at that time, the Portuguese in San Leandro produced almost all of their own food supply. They all kept gardens and fruit trees, almost all had a few milk cows which furnished milk and butter, and over half of them kept swine to help provide part of their meat. One noteworthy difference between Portuguese and American farmers was that "the former employ their countrymen practically to the exclusion of other races whether as regular or as temporary hands.[26] The process whereby Portuguese immigrants settled in San Leandro and gradually converted it into a Portuguese community is vividly described by one of the characters in Jack London's novel, *The Valley of the Moon*:

> Forty years ago Silva came from the Azores. Went sheep-herdin' in the mountains for a couple of years, then blew in to San Leandro. These five acres was the first land he leased. That was the beginnin'. Then he began leasin' by the hundreds of acres, an' by the hundred-an'-sixties. An' his sisters an' his uncles an' his aunts begun pourin' in from the Azores—they're all related there, you know; an' pretty soon San Leandro was a regular Porchugeeze settlement.[27]

The Central Valley of California also offered ample opportunities for the would-be farmer and the Portuguese responded to the challenge in a variety of ways. In 1888, John Avila introduced the sweet potato into the Atwater area of Merced County; it became a major commercial crop and he became known as the "father of the sweet potato industry."²⁸ By the beginning of the second decade of the 20th century, Portuguese farmers were noted growing strawberries near <u>Merced</u>, cherry orchards and asparagus in <u>Stockton</u>, sweet potatoes and pumpkins in an orchard in <u>Oakdale</u>, and lima beans in <u>Ventura</u>.²⁹ It was common knowledge at the time that, "As practical farmers, the Portuguese of the Pacific Coast, who were almost exclusively from the islands of the Azores, have few peers."³⁰ The most difficult obstacle to overcome for these immigrant farmers was acquiring enough land to enable them to become more than just subsistence farmers. Working someone else's land on a share basis or being a tenant farmer was the easiest way to start, but it offered little security. Every farmer wanted to own his own land, but it was not easy to accomplish. Looking back, one farmer's wife still remembered the constant struggle to become an independent farmer.

87

> I lived in Stevenson for eleven months after I got married. Then my husband's partner wanted to sell out and return to the old country. They sold out. My husband looked all over for a piece of ground. He finally found 20 acres here in Patterson (Stanislaus County) and we bought it for $11,000; it included eight cows and a small barn. We lived there for six years and then we bought the ten acres where this house is. My husband mortgaged the twenty acres that were clear then and joined a life insurance group to make sure that I wouldn't be left without anything if something should happen to him. Then we bought the twenty acres next to us and finally the next ten acres. I was unhappy when he bought the last ten acres because I thought we were never going to be out of debt. We finally ended up with sixty acres. It took us a long time to pay for it. It was just hard work and paying debts.³¹

Dairy Farming

The area just north of San Francisco, Marin County, is lacking in flat land suited for cultivation but possesses ideal conditions for raising livestock. It soon became known for its dairy farms, many of them specializing in producing butter. Some of the large landowners quickly discovered they could make better use of their holdings by dividing them into a number of small farms operated by tenant farmers on a share basis. The owner provided the fenced land, necessary buildings and cows while the tenant provided the dairy utensils, the needed horses and wagons, the furniture for the house, the farm implements, and the necessary labor. "The tenant pays to the owner twenty-seven-dollars-and-a-half per annum for each cow, and agrees to take the best care of the stock and of all parts of the farm; to make the necessary repairs, and to raise for the owner annually one-fifth as many calves as he keeps cows, the remainder of the calves being killed and fed to the pigs. He agrees also to sell nothing but butter and hogs from the farm, the hogs being entirely the tenant's property."[32]

To take over one of these dairy farms in 1870, a tenant needed about $2,000 and experience raising cows and pigs. A number of Portuguese became tenant dairy farmers—the experience they had, the capital they acquired. For those lacking the capital to operate a dairy farm themselves, there were always jobs available as hired hands. "The milkers and farm hands receive thirty dollars per month and 'found,' and good milkers are in constant demand."[33] Gradually, a pattern of movement evolved among Portuguese dairymen: young men would work as milkers on tenant farms operated by other Portuguese, not infrequently a relative or former acquaintance, until they could accumulate enough money to become tenant farmers themselves. At the same time, the tenant farmers were working to acquire enough capital to buy their own herd and dairy farm. The tenant farms of the San Francisco Bay area became a way station for many Portuguese who later became dairy farmers in the Central Valley of California.

The move toward the Central Valley after 1900 was at least partially motivated by the perceived opportunities there for dairymen. Most of the early Portuguese dairymen started out in Marin County, north of San Francisco, and gradually made the transition from milker to tenant farmer to owner. After the turn of the century, sheep-raising declined in the Central Valley as range land was divided up by irrigation canals and some of the Portuguese who had formerly tended sheep turned to dairy cows and irrigated pasture.[34] To help milk the cows and run the dairies, these Portuguese dairymen hired other Portuguese and encouraged relatives and friends from the Azores to join them. After a few years of milking cows and saving their money, many of these immigrants started their own dairies and, in turn, sent for more immigrants to join them. This self-perpetuating system reinforced the ties which existed between the immigrant population in California and the Azores by providing both destination and employment for friends and relatives anxious to leave the Azores, by furnishing a continuing supply of new labor for the expanding dairy industry, and by creating a growing class of entrepreneurs anxious to get started with their own dairies.

In many ways, the dairy industry was ideally suited for the Portuguese immigrants. Although they were poorly educated and had little knowledge of tools and machinery, they were skilled in raising and caring for livestock. Their inability to speak English made little difference in the daily life of running a dairy. Tied to the farm by the necessity of milking the animals both morning and night, they seldom needed to communicate with anyone other than hired hands, who inevitably were Portuguese themselves, and the cows, who produced milk regardless of what language the dairymen spoke. In addition, the initial investment needed to start a dairy was minimal. Other than the cows themselves, the necessary facilities could be rented or worked on a share basis until such time as enough land could be purchased to establish an owner-operated dairy. The dairy industry expanded rapidly in the Central Valley after 1910 and the initial success of Portuguese dairymen encouraged others to join them. In 1923, eighty-five percent of the dairymen in Merced and Stanislaus Counties were reported to be Portuguese, and by 1930 they were well established throughout the San Joaquin Valley dairy industry.[35]

The overwhelming success of Portuguese immigrants in the California dairy industry should not overshadow the fact that while many succeeded, many also failed. The day-to-day life of running a dairy, like any other business, was filled with challenges and difficulties. Some rose to the occasion, while others were not so fortunate. As one Portuguese dairy-farmer's wife recalled,

> My husband had five or six milkers—all Portuguese working on the dairy. When milking machines were introduced no one knew how to use them and they left them on the cows too long and ruined some of the cows. When the government started inspecting cows for T.B., in 1937, they took almost all of our cows—milkers and dry stock too— we were left with only eighteen cows. Everyone was so nervous, no one knew what to do. Each milker had only one or two cows to milk. It was a very serious time. We had to start building a new herd. We bought

ten big holsteins and the first one kicked a milking machine all apart. She had never had a machine on her before. It took a long time to try to rebuild the herd. A lot of dairies went out of business then.[36]

Following World War I, high wages offered for milkers attracted a number of Dutch and Portuguese immigrants to the dairy farms in the Los Angeles area. In the process of making the transition from milker to owner, they introduced an entirely new concept into the dairy industry of Southern California. Unable to purchase large land holdings to provide extensive pasture for their cattle, they kept them in corrals, as they had in their homeland, and brought feed to them. It soon became apparent that dairying on small units of land, based on a system of corral feeding, was both feasible and profitable.[37] This new technique of corral feeding, or dry-lot dairying as it came to be known, was rapidly copied by other dairy operators and by 1935, virtually the entire southern Los Angeles milkshed had been transformed into dry-lot dairying.[38] Portuguese dairymen eventually dominated the dairy industry in the San Joaquin Valley and became so associated with dairying throughout the state that the words "Portuguese" and "dairy farmer" became almost synonymous.

Settlement Patterns

By 1880, when the Portuguese foreign-born in California numbered 7,990, well over sixty percent were working as farmers or farm laborers and more than seventy percent of them were living in the Central Coast area[39] which stretches from San Luis Obispo County in the south to Sonoma County in the north. Sixty percent of the total were concentrated in the San Francisco-Oakland Bay Area and predominantly engaged in agricultural activities of one type or another. Although the other thirty percent were spread around the state, they too tended to be concentrated in a relatively small number of locations and occupations. The Sacramento Valley, which is in the northern third of the Central Valley, and particularly the area in the vicinity of Sacramento, accounted for about eleven percent of the total Portuguese population, with most of the working population engaged in agriculture. A smaller portion of the population was also occupied in fishing and urban-oriented jobs in the city. Gold mining was still an important occupation for a small

MAP 6

PORTUGUESE POPULATION IN CALIFORNIA, 1900

PORTUGUESE POPULATION IN CALIFORNIA, 1930

PORTUGUESE POPULATION IN CALIFORNIA, 1900

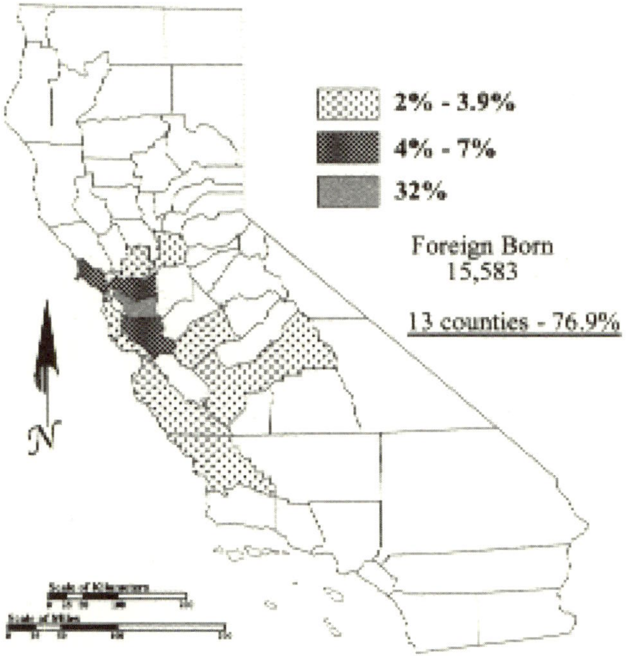

2% - 3.9%
4% - 7%
32%

Foreign Born
15,583

13 counties - 76.9%

PORTUGUESE POPULATION IN CALIFORNIA, 1930

2% - 3.9%
4% - 7%
8% - 10%
25.6%

Foreign Born
35,395

Foreign Stock
99,194

Total in 13 counties:
Foreign Born - 78.5%
Foreign Stock - 77.6%

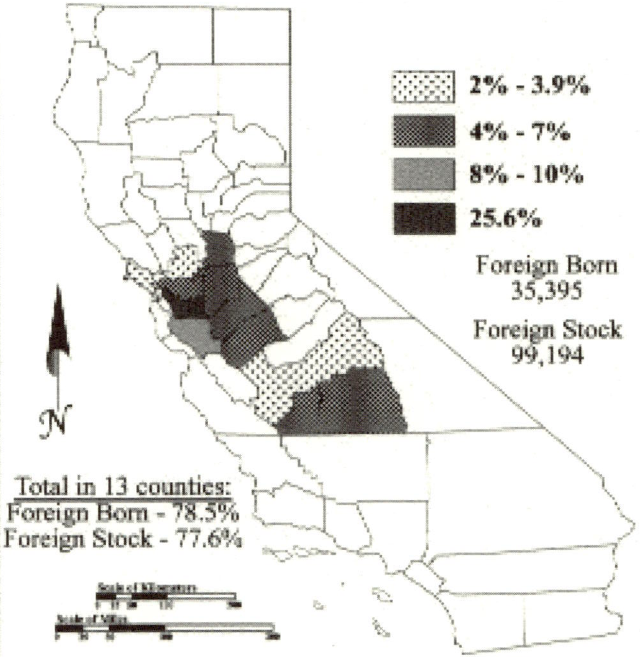

number of Portuguese immigrants in 1880; the largest concentrations were located in the major mining centers in the Sierra Nevada Mountains, while a lesser number could still be found in the northern part of the state. The San Joaquin Valley, which is in the southern two-thirds of the Central Valley, was notable for the number of its Portuguese sheep raisers and tenders as well as agriculturalists. Another minor concentration was located in Mendocino County along the North coast where they worked in the forestry industries. Southern California had the fewest Portuguese in 1880, with a small community of former shore-whalers living in the Los Angeles area and an active whaling group in Santa Barbara County."[40] Over half of all the Portuguese in the United States were living in California in 1880.[41] These new immigrants overwhelmingly chose agriculture as an occupation and Alameda County and the surrounding Bay Area as their preferred residential location.

Between 1880 and 1900, the number of foreign-born Portuguese in California almost doubled, but the general settlement pattern changed only slightly during this period. Thirty-two percent of the 15,583 foreign-born Portuguese living in California in 1900 could be found in Alameda County. Contra Costa County, on the north side of Alameda County, and Santa Clara County, on the south side, each accounted for another seven percent of the Portuguese immigrants, while Marin County, north of San Francisco, retained 5.2 percent and San Francisco County 3.9 percent. Together those five Bay Area counties were home to fifty-five percent of all the foreign-born Portuguese in California in 1900 and were at the core of a predominantly coastal pattern of distribution concentrated between Marin County in the north and San Luis Obispo County in the south (see Map 6).

In 1900, the 15,583 foreign-born Portuguese in California represented 32.4 percent of the nation's total. California's population of Portuguese immigrants doubled again by 1920 when they numbered 33,025.[42] After 1920, new and more restrictive immigration laws, together with worsening economic conditions for United States farmers, brought new immigration to a virtual standstill and provided the incentive for a substantial return migration of disenchanted immigrants. At the close of the second stage of migration in 1930, California's foreign-born Portuguese population totaled 35,395 and their offspring numbered another 63,799, with a total of 99,194. These foreign-born Portuguese constituted 32.4 percent of the nation's total—the exact same percentage found in the state in 1900. Within California, however, a major change had occurred in the location and occupation of the Portuguese population in the course of thirty years. While Alameda County still represented the single largest concentration of Portuguese in the state, its share had declined to 25.6 percent. More importantly, the general focus of Portuguese settlement had shifted away from the Central Coast and to the Central Valley of California. An eight-county area in the Central Valley, consisting of Solano and Sacramento on the north end, King and Tulare on the south, and the four counties in between, which accounted for slightly more than ten percent of the foreign-born Portuguese population in 1900 when the state's total was 15,583, now represented thirty-five percent of the state's 35,395 Portuguese immigrants (see Map 6).

93

The Human Side

Viewed collectively, the migration experience of a people frequently obscures the heartaches of dislocation, the fear of the unknown, the hardships and struggles involved in starting life anew, and the joys and sorrows that are a part of everyday living for immigrants and non-immigrants alike. The most difficult aspect of a collective migration to capture and appreciate is the effect that the experience had on the individuals involved. The real-life experience of a single individual as related by a descendent, while not typical—in the sense that there is no such thing as a typical immigrant—illustrates the human side of the Azorean migration to California and the United States. This story, related by the son of an immigrant, brings to life those experiences.

Manuel A. was born in the Azores on the island of Terceira in 1869 and was working as an errand boy when he decided to come to America to avoid being drafted into the Portuguese army. In 1889, some men hid him with the trunks in a cargo ship and he came to America as a stowaway on a sailing ship. It took him thirty-seven days to reach the United States. The first year he was in this country he worked in a lumber mill in Vermont for $20 a month, but it was awfully cold and he didn't like it. He decided to go to California where he had an older brother and ended up in San Francisco at the Portuguese Hotel. He stayed there until he got a job working in the lumber mills in Humboldt County at $25 a month. He saved his money and soon went into partnership with his brother in a small dairy where they separated the cream from the milk, sold the cream, and fed the skim-milk to hogs. They raised their own vegetables, including potatoes, and butchered a hog when they needed meat; they only went to town twice a year to buy staples and supplies. The partnership lasted twelve years when they decided to sell out and Manuel returned to the Azores to see his mother.

When he was preparing to leave for the Azores, in 1905, a Portuguese woman in Arcadia asked him to take a few things back to her parents and sister who also lived in Terceira. He ended up marrying the woman's sister and they had four children in the Azores but two of them—both girls— died of dysentery. After six years Dad realized that he could never be able to make a sufficient living in the Azores so he decided to return to America before he ran out of money. He left the Azores, for the second time, with his wife and two boys in 1911. This time the trip was made by steamship and took only seven days. One of the two boys got sick coming over and never fully recovered; he died after they reached Califomia.

From the East Coast the family traveled to California by train. It was a tiring, seven-day trip across the country. Seven weary days of dirt from the soot and ashes of the train, and of caring for a sick boy. They returned to Arcadia where Mom's sister lived, but the area did not seem to offer much promise and after the boy died they moved to Gustine (Stanislaus County) where Dad's older brother had been since 1905 and Dad went back into partnership with him. We lived in Gustine for three years and E. was born there in 1912. From there we moved to Turlock (Stanislaus County) where Dad bought a twenty-acre farm. We stayed there for three years and J. was born there in 1916. Afterwards we moved to Ceres (Stanislaus County) where Dad operated a dairy on a share basis until 1925 when he bought a dairy in Salida (Stanislaus County). Mom came down sick about a year after J. was born and had a major operation. Two years after we moved to Salida, Mom died at the age of forty-nine. E. was fifteen then and had to take over the housekeeping duties. She had finished grammar school but she never went back to school.

In addition to the dairy, Dad raised melons, pumpkins, potatoes and vegetables of all kinds. What we didn't eat or give away was fed to the pigs.

Times were difficult in the 1920s and 1930s. We raised most of our own food and we did without a lot of things. We received a new outfit of clothes once a year and the rest of the year the clothes were patched and repatched. There were few luxuries. E. took care of the house and M., the older brother, and J. helped on the dairy and worked part-time for the neighbors when they could.

In 1925, an epidemic of hoof-and-mouth disease broke out in the valley and all the infected cows had to be destroyed. It was especially bad in the Fresno, Merced and Gustine areas and everyone was under a great deal of pressure because they were afraid that it would hit their cows. Everyone was worried about the disease and when we went to school we had to dip our shoes in sheep dip—a disinfectant—when we arrived and when we left to go home. Some people had nervous breakdowns because they lost all their herd. It was a dreadful time. We didn't have any cows come down with it, but Dad was really worried. One day the dog followed our horses when a neighbor borrowed them and when the dog came back he was tired-out and had saliva dripping from his mouth. Dad was so afraid that the dog might have hoof-and-mouth disease and the dairy would end up quarantined and the cows killed that he killed our dog—the best dog we ever had. Dad was under a lot of tension.

We always spoke Portuguese at home. Dad could read and write English but Mom never learned any English. Mom never had the opportunity to go to school in the Azores, but Dad taught her how to sign her name. Dad received a Portuguese language newspaper from Oakland and used to read to Mom. When we lived in Ceres, the landlord used to teach us some English words; other than that we didn't know any English before we started to school. The old-timers thought it was more important for the children to help work at home than to go to school and get an education. You didn't need an education to farm; you needed to learn how to work and to farm. Dad kept M. out of school a lot to help with the work on the dairy and he didn't get much formal education. He also kept J. out of school to help. One day the truant officer came to our house and threatened to arrest Dad if he kept J. out of school one more time. The combination of trying to learn the language, moving several times, and missing a lot of school resulted in our repeating grades.

Dad never became a citizen. He was still afraid a war might break out and he would get called—that was the reason why he left the Azores.

Mother never became a citizen either. Dad joined the UPEC [a fraternal organization for men] after he came back to California with his family and Mom belonged to the SPRSI [a fraternal organization for women]. Both provided insurance benefits for their members. Dad sold the dairy cows in 1934 and leased the ranch. He died in 1942 at the age of 73.

Hawaii

Proximity to the Azores was certainly not one of the attributes of the Hawaiian Islands. Just getting there entailed a journey one-third of the way around the world. And yet, by 1900, sixteen percent of the foreign-born Portuguese population of the United States and its territories were living in these islands. This sudden rise in the Portuguese population of the Hawaiian Islands is noteworthy both for the rapidity and the manner in which it occurred.

Prior to 1870, there were only about 400 Portuguese living in the islands. Virtually all of them were remnants, in one way or another, of the whaling era. From the 1840s, until whaling began its sharp decline in the 1870s, the Pacific whaling grounds were the major source of whales for the American fleet. During that time, and particularly after the discovery of gold in California, the Hawaiian Islands flourished as the principal outfitting and transshipment center for the Pacific whaling fleet. The large numbers of Azoreans engaged in whaling made it inevitable that many would come in contact with the Hawaiian Islands and that some would end up there permanently. Some deserted their ships and chose to remain in the islands when the whalers, laden with oil and bone, set sail for their homeport in New England. The continuing shortage of crewmen made it easy to sign on with another ship headed for the whaling grounds, and the islands, so similar to their homeland were, for many, preferable to the long journey back to the unfamiliar climate of New England. With the gradual decline of whaling, the Portuguese who remained in the islands reverted to a lifestyle more typical of their homeland.

With its rich volcanic soils and tropical climate, Hawaii possessed two of the three basic ingredients necessary to develop and sustain a substantial sugar cane industry. The only thing lacking was a continuous supply of cheap labor. To solve that problem the government, in conjunction with the plantation owners, turned to immigration from abroad. Chinese men were the first group to come to Hawaii to work in the canefields in any substantial numbers, but the government was unsuccessful in its efforts to attract Chinese women to the islands. The arrival of large numbers of single Chinese males soon aroused a negative reaction among the general population of the islands and the plantation owners and government began to cast about in search of a source of family immigrants as a long-term solution to the need for plantation workers. The former whalers from the Azores and Madeira Islands had, for the most part, turned to agriculture by the 1870s, either on their own small farms or as workers on the plantations and ranches on the islands, and had proven themselves to be industrious workers.[44]

A former resident of Hawaii, ever alert to the planters' need for cheap labor and the opportunity to benefit personally from that need, made a strong case for importing Portuguese immigrants to solve the labor problem in the islands. In a letter from the Madeira Islands in 1876, he wrote:

> In my opinion your islands could not possibly get a more desirable class of immigrants than the population of the Madeira and Azore Islands. Sober, honest, industrious and peaceable, they combine all the qualities of a good settler and with all this, they are inured to your climate. Their education and ideas of comfort and social requirements are just low enough to make them content with the lot of an isolated settler and its attendant privations, while on the other hand their mental capabilities and habits of work will ensure them a much higher status in the next generation ...[45]

The Portuguese, to all appearances, were ideal candidates for the cane fields and serious negotiations were soon initiated. When the final agreements were completed in 1877, the Board of Immigration for the Hawaiian Islands had agreed to incur the cost of transportation for immigrants and their families from the Madeira and Azores and to provide them with jobs at $10 per month, lodging, rations and medical care. On their part, the Portuguese immigrants were required to sign a contract agreeing to work on the plantations for ninety-six months. Withdrawing from the contract, or failure to comply with it after reaching Hawaii, obligated the immigrant to reimburse the Board for the cost of his passage.

The first Portuguese immigrants arrived in Honolulu in 1878. Between then and 1899, twenty-one ships deposited 12,780 Madeiran and Azorean Islanders in Hawaii.[46] Eleven of the twenty-one were sailing vessels and for them it was a long, slow trip from the eastern Atlantic Ocean, around Cape Horn and on to the Hawaiian Islands. One of the 400 passengers sailing on the ship *Thomas Bell* in 1887 kept a daily journal of the <u>156 day trip</u>. His remarkable account recreates in microcosm the experiences of many of the Portuguese immigrants bound for Hawaii: rough seas, disease, deaths, births, marriages, becalmed seas, food shortages, infestations of bedbugs, stormy weather, fights between passengers and crew and among the passengers themselves, boredom, promiscuity, the Christmas season, dancing, fishing, and waiting—such was their lot.[47]

Portuguese immigrants in Hawaii found themselves in a somewhat different position, vis-a-vis the dominant social group, than did their counterparts in Massachusetts and Rhode Island. On the East Coast of the continental United States, the Portuguese were just one of a myriad of ethnic groups pouring into the country. And if they were poor, spoke a foreign language, and had different customs, they were generically indistinguishable from millions of other immigrants who were also poor, spoke a foreign language, and adhered to different customs. Although the Portuguese who entered the Hawaiian Islands after 1878 were grudgingly acknowledged as "Caucasians" in a Caucasian-dominated society, they were in the unfortunate position of having arrived in large numbers, possessing few worldly goods, and, as contract labor, occupying the absolute bottom of the economic ladder. They quickly came to be looked down upon as "an inferior people of low economic and social status."[48] The connotation of farm laborer or independent agriculturalist was quite different in the diversified economy of the continental United States than it was in the plantation economy of Hawaii where agricultural workers were at the very bottom of the social system. The negative association of agriculture and social status quickly became apparent to the Portuguese immigrants and they reacted in a variety of ways, almost all of which served to put as much distance as possible, either physical or social, between themselves and other contract laborers. Many completely removed themselves from the islands by migrating to the mainland. Between 1911 and 1914, for example, over two thousand relocated in California.[49] Others "worked their way urbanward as fast as possible to escape the stigma attached to lowly plantation labor and to better their economic conditions ..."[50]

The family story of Cecelia P. aptly illustrates the Portuguese experience in Hawaii. Her paternal grandfather, Frank, was born on São Miguel. As a teenager, he and two older brothers left the Azores as emigrants in the 1870s. One brother ended up in Providence, Rhode Island, the other went to Brazil, and Frank signed a three-year contract to go to Hawaii where he was employed as a sugar plantation carpenter on the big island of Hawaii. He met his future wife, also from the Azores, in Hawaii where they were married and had a large family. John P., one of the children of that family, grew up on the sugar plantation where his father worked. Cecelia P.'s maternal grandparents were from the Madeira Islands. They were among the earliest immigrants recruited from those islands to work as sugar plantation laborers on the big island of Hawaii. Their first child was born on the ship that brought them from Madeira to Hawaii. Their daughter, Maria C., was born and grew up on a sugar plantation in Hawaii. The parents of John P. and Maria C. all lived and worked on the same sugar plantation where the children grew up together and eventually married. When Cecelia P. was born in 1912, her father worked in the mill on that same sugar plantation. He moved to a small sugar plantation as manager in 1919 and finally, in 1925, to the city of Hilo, Hawaii where he was employed as a maintenance person at the city hospital. Living in Hilo, the largest city on the big island of Hawaii, enabled Cecelia P. to get a high school education and attend the University of Hawaii for two years. As a young woman, Cecelia P. worked as a receptionist for a new young Chinese doctor in Hilo, Hawaii and they were eventually married.[51]

Of the 12,780 Portuguese immigrants who arrived between 1878 and 1899, forty-two percent were men, nineteen percent women, and thirty-nine percent children. The Census of 1900, taken just two years after Hawaii was annexed to the United States in July, 1898, recorded 7,668 foreign-born Portuguese in the islands,[52] most of them relatively new arrivals. Between 1906 and 1909, three more steamships arrived with an additional 3,314 immigrants, thereby raising the total number of Portuguese who immigrated as contract laborers to 16,094.[53] In marked contrast to the Portuguese on the East Coast of the United States, who collectively reinforced their cultural heritage and maintained their ethnic identity, Portuguese immigrants in Hawaii disbanded as a nationality group, settled apart from one another and preferably, in *haole*-occupied areas. They associated with others outside their own group, modifying old-world customs and taking on new ones, marrying outside the group and especially into the *haole* group, giving up old-world institutions and languages, even changing their names in some instances—anything and everything was justified in order to obliterate the *haole* stereotype of a "Portagee."[54]

100

Initially brought in as laborers for the sugar cane plantations, the early settlement pattern of Portuguese immigrants coincided with the sugar-producing islands. By 1900, however, the total Portuguese foreign-born population had declined to 7,668 and was concentrated primarily on the island of Oahu, Honolulu County, with 38.1 percent of the total, and the big island of Hawaii, with 35.6 percent (see Map 7). On the mainland, new immigrants continued to arrive until they were slowed down by the literacy requirement of 1917 and then shut out by the National Origin's legislation of the 1920s. After the Hawaiian Islands discontinued sponsoring contract labor from the Madeira and Azores in the first decade of the 20th century, the flow of Portuguese immigration to that part of the United States ceased. As previously noted, a reverse flow of Portuguese out-migration from the Hawaiian Islands to the mainland replaced the earlier immigration. Instead of encouraging friends and relatives to join them in the Hawaiian Islands, the immigrants utilized their social networks to advise other potential immigrants to go elsewhere and, in fact, to make contact on the mainland so they themselves could leave the islands.

According to the Census of 1930, there were 15,048 individuals classified as Portuguese "foreign stock" living in the Hawaiian Islands. Only 3,713 of those, however, were foreign-born. The relocation within the islands, first noticeable in 1900, became even more accentuated by 1930 when over fifty percent of both the Portuguese foreign-born and "foreign stock" were concentrated in Honolulu County on the island of Oahu. The most obvious decline in the percentage of Portuguese living in the islands was registered by the big island of Hawaii which wentfrom

MAP 7

PORTUGUESE POPULATION OF HAWAII, 1900

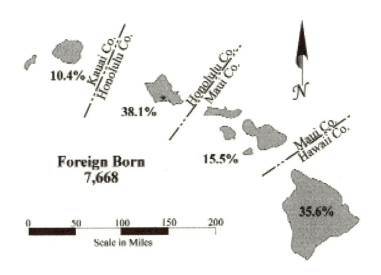

Source: Twelfth Census of the United States, 1900, Vol. II Population, Part 2.

PORTUGUESE POPULATION OF HAWAII, 1930

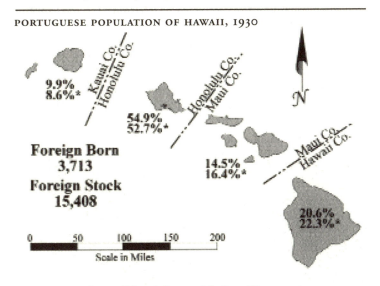

Source: Fifteenth Census of the United States, 1930. Outlying Territories and Possessions.

35.6 percent of the foreign-born in 1900 to 20.6 percent in 1930 (see Map 7). Although the total foreign-born Portuguese population of the Hawaiian Islands declined after 1900, the size of the original immigrant population imported into the islands as contract laborers, together with their offspring, was sufficiently large to maintain Hawaii's position as one of the major concentrations of Portuguese in the United States and its territories through the mid-1900s.

The apparent success in attracting Portuguese families to immigrate to Hawaii was tempered by the expense of the program; the long voyage from the Madeira and Azores together with the high percentage of children resulted in a high cost per working immigrant. After complying with the terms of their contract, many of the early immigrants took advantage of their relative proximity to the West Coast of the continental United States and moved on to California. Some of the later arrivals left almost immediately for California.[55] The planters and government soon came to the conclusion that the liabilities of sponsoring Portuguese immigration were greater than the benefits and began to seek a supply of cheap labor closer to home. Their subsequent success in attracting cane-field workers from Japan brought a close to the importation of Portuguese as contract laborers to Hawaii.

*

Between 1870 and 1900, two noticeable changes occurred in the Portuguese population of the United States. The first was a substantial increase in the absolute number of Portuguese, and the second was the sudden appearance of a significant Portuguese immigrant population in the Hawaiian Islands. The 8,605 foreign-born Portuguese enumerated by the Census of 1870 had increased to 48,099 thirty years later. The relative distribution in 1900 closely followed the pattern that was well established by 1870. Massachusetts, California and Rhode Island accounted for 75.5 percent of the foreign-born Portuguese in the United States with an additional 15.9 percent located in Hawaii. These four political entities together represented 91.4 percent of all the foreign-born Portuguese in the United States in 1900.

By 1930, the number of foreign-born Portuguese in the United States and its possessions exceeded 100,000 for the first time and when

FIGURE 2

PORTUGUESE POPULATION BY STATE – 1870-1930

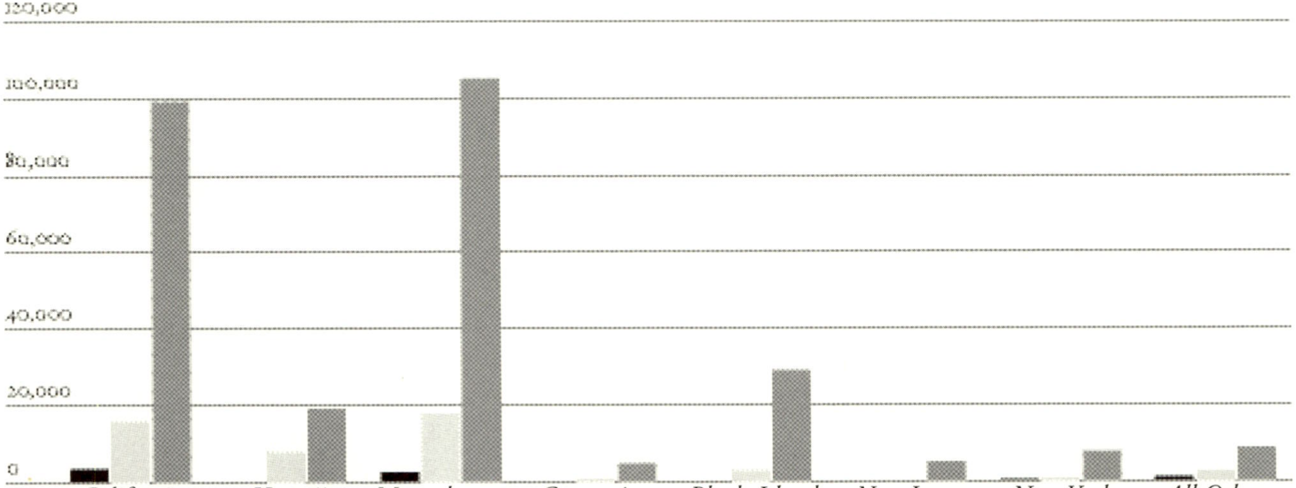

	California	Hawaii	Massachusetts	Connecticut	Rhode Island	New Jersey	New York	All Others	Totals
1870	3,435		2,555	221	189		334	1,015	4,314
1900	15,583	7,668	17,885	655	2,865	62	823	2,558	48,099
1930	99,194	19,121	105,076	4,701	29,097	5,099	7,758	8,680	278,726

SOURCE: UNITED STATES IMMIGRATION AND NATURALIZATION SERVICE

their American-born offspring were included, the total reached 278,726. The pattern of distribution, however, changed very little from 1900. Massachusetts, California, Rhode Island and Hawaii still accounted for 90.5 percent of all Portuguese "foreign stock." Hawaii and Rhode Island did switch relative ranks between 1900 and 1930; Rhode Island continued to attract Portuguese immigrants until the mid-1920s, but few Portuguese migrated to the Hawaiian Islands after 1900. Instead, there was a noticeable out-migration of Portuguese immigrants from Hawaii to California. The relative concentration of Portuguese remained, however, within the same four states (see Figure 2).

Notes

[1] Contrary to popular mythology, California was not an unknown land that sprang into existence with the discovery of gold in 1848 and the subsequent invasion by the '49ers. Although João Cabrilho, a Portuguese captain, is credited with discovering California for the Europeans in 1542, he was under the employ of the Spanish crown. Furthermore, another three hundred years elapsed before the first permanent Portuguese settler arrived in California. Part of the Spanish Empire until 1822, when Mexico gained its independence, only the coastal area of California was occupied by these would-be conquistadors. Unable to find large concentrations of either Indians or wealth they turned their interest to grazing cattle on the extensive holdings of natural range. Even so, California was not unknown to the inhabitants of the East Coast of the United States. Although direct trade with foreigners was prohibited in Spain's colonies, contra-band fur traders from Massachusetts had frequented the coast of California since before the turn of the 19th century. After Mexico gained its independence, merchant seamen out of Massachusetts frequented the coastal areas to trade their merchandise for California cowhides in the 1830s and '40s. California life in this period is vividly described by John Henry Dana in *Two Years Before the Mast.* In his trip to California (1834-36), Dana encountered "Massachusetts men established all along the Coast, from a one-eyed Fall River whaleman tending bar in a San Diego *pulqeria,* to Thomas O. Larkin, the merchant prince of Monterey." John Henry Dana, *Two Years Before the Mast: A Personal Narrative of Life at Sea.* (New York, 1936), 30-46. Those cowhides, known as California cartwheels, helped supply the needed raw materials for the New England shoe factories in the 19th century. After New Bedford whalers started working the Pacific whaling grounds in the late 1830s, they frequently stopped along the California coast for fresh beef.

[2] It was not until António Silva arrived in 1840 that the first Portuguese whaler deserted his ship to take up life in California.

[3] J.T. Jenkins, *A History of the Whale Fisheries,* (New York, 1971), 234.

[4] A. Starbuck, *History of the American Whale Fishery from Its Earliest Inception to the Year 1876,* 2 vols. (New York, 1964), 112.

[5] Ibid. By the end of the 1850s, whaling ships were forced to pay advance wages as an inducement to recruit seamen for their crews. Even so, the fleet was plagued with bounty-jumpers who took the advance pay and deserted at the first opportunity. "There were times, when the California fever was at its highest, that the desertions did not stop with the men, but officers and even captains seem to vie with the crew" in leaving their ships.

[6] S.E. Morison, *The Maritime History of Massachusetts 1783-1860,* (New York, 1921), 333.

[7] J. Walton, *A Historical Study of the Portuguese in California,* (San Francisco, 1972), 51.

[8] Allyn C. Loosley, "Foreign Born Population of California." (MA Thesis, University of California, Berkeley, 1927), 5.

[9] *Eighth Census of the United States, 1860.* Vol. 1.

[10] Alvin Graves, "Immigrants in Agriculture: The Portuguese Californians, 1850-1970s," (Ph.D. dissertation, University of California, Los Angeles, 1977), 49.

[11] Edwin C. Starks, *A History of California Shore Whaling,* (Sacramento, 1922), 17.

[12] C.M. Scammon, *The Marine Mammals of the North-Western Coast of North America,* (San Francisco, 1874), 250.

[13] Starks, *A History of California Shore Whaling,* 20.

[14] George Brown Goode, *The Fisheries and Fishery Industry of the United States,* Vol. V, Part II, (Washington, DC, 1887), 55.

[15] L. Oliver, *Never Backward: The Autobiography of Lawrence Oliver—A Portuguese-American,* (San Diego, 1972), 23 -24.

[16] Frederick G. Williams, "Os Inícios da Pesca do Atum em San Diego" in *First Symposium on Portuguese Presence in California,* (San Francisco, 1974), 7.

[17] H. C. Godsil, *The High Seas Tuna Fishery of California,* (Sacramento, 1938), 17.

[18] Michael K. Orbach, *Hunters, Seamen and Entrepreneurs: The Tuna Seinermen of San Diego,* (Berkeley, 1977), 7.

[19] Forest Crissey, *Where Opportunity Knocks Twice,* (Chicago, 1914), 74-75.

[20] U.S. Congress, "Portuguese Farmers About San Leandro, California." in *Immigrant Farmers in the Western States.* Senate Report of the U.S. Immigration Commission, Vol. 24, Pt. II, (Washington, DC: U.S. Government Printing Office, 1911), 491.

[21] Graves, "Immigrants in Agriculture: The Portuguese Californians, 1850-1970s," 50-51.

[22] William Halley, *The Centennial Year Book of Alameda County, California,* (Oakland, 1876), 292-93.

[23] Ibid., 198.

[24] United States Congress, Senate Report of the U.S. Immigration Commission, Vol. 24, Part II, *Immigrant Farmers in the Western States,* Chapter XIV, (Washington, DC, 1911), 490.

[25] Ibid., 490-91.

[26] Jack London, *The Valley of the Moon,* (New York, 1914).

[27] Manoel da Silveira Cardozo, *The Portuguese in America 590 B.C.-1974,* (New York, 1976), 37.

[28] F. Crissey, *Where Opportunity Knocks Twice,* (Chicago, 1914), 78-81.

[29] Ibid., 59.

[30] Interview with Alexandrina Alves in Patterson, California, on Nov. 25, 1978.

[31] Charles Nordhoff, *Northern California, Oregon, and the Sandwich Islands,* (New York, 1874), 180.

[32] Ibid., 181.

[33] Crissey, *Where Opportunity Knocks Twice,* 68-71.

[34] Graves, "Immigrants in Agriculture: The Portuguese Californians, 1850-1970s," 120.

[35] Interview with Maria B. Diniz in Patterson, California, on Nov. 25, 1978.

[36] John G. Gielding, "Dairying in the Los Angeles Milkshed: Factors Affecting Character and Location," (Ph.D. dissertation, University of California at Los Angeles), 32.

[37] Ibid., 69.

[38] Graves, "Immigrants in Agriculture: The Portuguese Californians, 1850-1970s," 52-53.

[39] Ibid., 58-62.

[40] Ibid.

[41] *Fourteenth Census of the United States, 1920,* Vol. 3.

[42] Interview with Elsie (Avila) Maciel and John Avila in Modesto, California, on Nov. 24, 1978.

[43] Ralph S. Kuykendall, *The Hawaiian Kingdom, Vol.III, 1874-1893,* The Kalakaua Dynasty . (Honolulu, 1967), 119-122.

[44] Ibid., 123.

[45] João Baptista d'Oliveira and Vincente d'Ornellas, "Destination, Sandwich Islands, Nov. 8, 1887." Lucile de Silva Canario (trans.) in *The Hawaiian Journal of History,* Vol. 4 (1970): 49-51.

[46] Ibid., 3 -50.

[47] Gerald Allan Estep, "Social Placement of the Portuguese in Hawaii as Indicated by Factors in Assimilation," (MA Thesis, University of Southern California, 1941), 16.

[48] Gerald Allen Estep, "Portuguese Assimilation in Hawaii and California," *Sociology and Social Research* 26, (1941): 61-8.

[49] Ibid., 62.

[50] Muncel Chang, Unpublished family history, 2002.

[51] *Twelfth Census of the United States, 1900,* Vol. 2, Part 2, (Washington, D.C., 1900).

[52] Baptista d'Oliveira and d'Ornellas, Destination, Sandwich Islands, Nov. 8, 1887," 51-52.

[53] Estep, "Portuguese Assimilation in Hawaii and California," 67.

[54] Nancy F. Young (compiler), *The Portuguese in Hawaii: A Resource Guide,* (Honolulu, 1973).

CHAPTER IV

THE NEW IMMIGRANTS

The Thirty Year Interlude

The Portuguese migrants who arrived in the United States during the 1920s found that economic conditions in their new homeland were not as promising as anticipated. The depression that first affected farmers in the late 1920s worsened and became widespread during the 1930s. Although they were not unaccustomed to hard times, most of the Azorean immigrants were inexperienced in surviving in a depressed urban-industrial environment.

The increasing unionization of the textile industry in New England, together with the growing obsolescence of much of the original mill equipment, made that industry particularly susceptible to competition from modern textile mills located in the South with its low-cost, non-union labor. As the economic realities of the industry became more apparent, some mill owners closed their New England plants and joined the move to the South in search of cheap labor. Others tried to forestall the impending crisis by cutting wages in their existing plants. The workers, caught in the middle of a situation that they neither created nor understood, reacted by striking. In the textile mills of New Bedford, for example—and they were by no means atypical—management announced a ten percent wage cut in 1928 and the mill workers reacted by going out on strike. The strike lasted six months, the longest and most severe strike in the city's history, and only succeeded in aggravating a deteriorating situation.[1]

Already reeling under the intense competition from the South, the depression of the 1930s dealt the textile industry of New England the final blow. New Bedford lost two-thirds of its cotton textile mills during the depression and became "a typical example of a depressed one-industry city."[2] The number of workers employed in cotton textiles in New Bedford between 1927 and 1938 decreased by 21,280.[3] Hampered by their lack of education and delayed acquisition of English, "fully ninety-one percent of their [Portuguese] workers were found in the semi-skilled and unskilled occupations"[4] which bore the brunt of the layoffs and job terminations that swept the New England textile industries during the 1930s. Ill-prepared to compete on the open job market, the Portuguese suffered from high rates of unemployment. Half of the Portuguese working population of New Bedford, for example, were left without jobs during the 1930s[5] and "[t]he movement of cotton manufacturing to the South ... created in New England (in such cities as New Bedford, Fall River and Lowell, and especially in the smaller towns) a serious problem of a more or less permanently 'stranded population'..."[6] Portuguese workers were particularly conspicuous in that "stranded population" and were hard hit by the economic downturn.

At the same time that the textile industry was relocating to the South, the garment industry of New York City was trying to escape their increasing labor costs. Historically dependent upon low-cost, unskilled, immigrant labor, the garment industry was affected by the decline in new immigrants after 1924 and viewed their rising labor costs with apprehension. New York City's importance as the fashion center of the United States dictated that the garment industry, while not tied exclusively to the city, remain in relatively close proximity. Lower production costs in New Jersey and Connecticut and the increasing pool of unemployed workers in southern Massachusetts stimulated a substantial migration of the garment industry from New York City to those areas after the late 1920s. By 1938, New Bedford was the third-ranking employer, in terms of total number of employees, in the clothing industry.[7]

During this period, many Portuguese immigrants who had previously worked in the textile mills sought employment in the garment industry. Unskilled and uneducated, they were ideal candidates for the low-paying job of mass-producing clothing. Even so, the new industry was not able to substantially reduce unemployment among Portuguese workers in Fall River and New Bedford and "many of them moved to

FIGURE 3

PORTUGUESE POPULATION BY STATE, 1900-1990

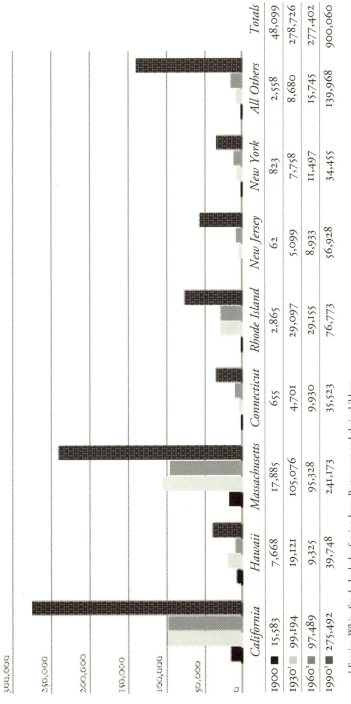

	California	Hawaii	Massachusetts	Connecticut	Rhode Island	New Jersey	New York	All Others	Totals
1900	15,583	7,668	17,885	655	2,865	62	823	2,558	48,099
1930[1]	99,194	19,121	105,076	4,701	29,097	5,099	7,758	8,680	278,726
1960[2]	97,489	9,325	95,328	9,930	29,155	8,933	11,497	15,745	277,402
1990[3]	275,492	39,748	241,173	35,523	76,773	56,928	34,455	139,968	900,060

[1] Foreign White Stock. Includes foreign born Portuguese and their children.
[2] Census of the Population, 1960 Vol. I. Characteristics of the Population. Part I
[3] Census of the Population, 1990 (Portuguese primary ancestors)

Newark, New Jersey, and other cities in search of jobs."[8] The early stages of the migration from Massachusetts to Connecticut and New Jersey were already apparent in the Census of 1930 (see Figure 3). These early migrants, like their predecessors who first came to America, established themselves in urban occupations and provided a destination and assistance to subsequent waves of migration during the thirties.

The economic malaise which settled on the New England textile centers in the 1920s slowed the occupational progress of its newest immigrant groups to a standstill. This was particularly true for the Portuguese in places like Fall River and New Bedford, where that progress has remained stalled to the present.[9] In addition to making it difficult to maintain family and community stability, the loss of jobs and continued unemployment had a negative impact upon traditional Portuguese cultural values among some members of the community who came to associate "being Portuguese" with being unemployable or somehow inferior to being American. The move to disassociate themselves, at least from the more visible signs of their cultural heritage, such as speaking Portuguese, became more commonplace.

Hard on the heels of the economic collapse of the 1930s came World War II. While it solved the job shortage and put the nation back to work, it created other pressures, particularly for ethnic minorities. World War II, even more than the previous war, was a war for ideological and political survival. As such, it required Herculean efforts on the part of the inhabitants of the United States to supply men and equipment in sufficient quantities to wage a war. In the "us" versus "them" psychology of total warfare, there was little room for the non-committed. Under the guise of patriotism, many former immigrants abandoned their native tongue, anglicized their name, and de-emphasized "un-American" cultural traditions. The pressure to be a "100 percent American" during the war years was most pronounced in urban settings, where there was greater day-to-day contact between immigrants and nonimmigrants, whereas the isolation of rural life tended to diffuse the impact of many immediate, short-term side effects of the war effort. As one researcher commented in 1949, "many Portuguese immigrants and their children have leaned toward discarding the Portuguese language, not only in order to conceal their background as a means of overcoming social prejudices, but also in order to fulfill what they consider a patriotic duty."[10]

The flow of Portuguese immigrants to the United States never completely ceased after the restrictive legislation of the early 1920s was enacted, but it came close during the depression years of the 1930s. During that decade, only 3,329 Portuguese immigrants arrived in this country, which was fewer than 350 per year. In the ten years that followed, 7,423 managed to migrate to the United States, less than 750 per year.[11] Without any substantial input from new immigrants, cultural reinforcement lessened with each passing year. The minimal cultural impact of 10,722 new immigrants in twenty years is even more apparent when compared to the base population of 278,726 inhabitants of Portuguese "foreign stock" residing in the United States in 1930. Economic and social pressures combined to force conformity toward some preconceived model of an American citizen. The absence of any large-scale immigration of people exemplifying traditional cultural values of the Azores greatly facilitated the dual process of acculturation and assimilation. The social networks suffered from reduced contact between inhabitants of the islands and the United States during the thirty-year interlude, but still continued to connect the two populations.

Reopening the Gates—The Third Stage of Immigration

Economic conditions continued to improve in the United States during the 1950s and, at the same time, worsened in the Azores. This increasing gap created the dynamics that led to the renewed immigration from the Azores. The first significant resumption of Portuguese immigration to the United States developed out of a natural disaster in the Azores. In 1957, the island of Faial was shaken by the eruption of a new volcano and, although no lives were lost, a considerable amount of damage occurred in one of the more isolated villages and the surrounding area. During the post-World War II years, the United States developed a "refugee tradition" and special legislation was enacted time and time again to permit a non-quota flow of immigrants into the United States to allow them to escape a difficult situation in their homeland. True to form, Congress enacted the Azorean Refugee Act of 1958 and 1960, which marked the beginnings of the third stage of migration from the Azores to the United States. To help ease the problems of resettlement caused by the volcanic eruption, Congress first created 1,500 special non-quota visas to enable heads of family from Faial to immigrate to the United States. In 1960, 2,000 additional non-quota visas were authorized. In all, 4,811 Portuguese immigrated to the United States under the Azorean Refugee Acts.[12] The volcanic eruptions also aroused a great deal of sympathy from Portuguese-Americans for relatives still living in the islands and they assisted refugees from the natural disaster on Faial to secure employment and housing.

Although immigration under the refugee acts was restricted to people affected by the eruption of the volcano on Faial, the acts were followed in the mid-1960s by a complete revision of the immigration laws of the United States. The National Origins' Legislation of the 1920s was replaced with less restrictive and non-discriminatory quotas and authorized a substantial increase in the number of immigrants permitted to enter the United States from all foreign countries. The new law provided:

112

> the admission of immediate relatives (unmarried children under twenty-one, spouse, and parents of a U.S. citizen) without numerical limitations. It further allows a maximum of 20,000 visas to each Eastern Hemisphere country, preference to be given to unmarried adult sons or daughters of U.S. citizens, then to spouses and unmarried sons or daughters of permanent resident aliens, then to married sons or daughters of U.S. citizens, then to brothers or sisters of U.S. citizens, and finally to nonpreference immigrants.[13]

The revision of U.S. immigration laws could not have come at a more opportune time for the severely overpopulated Azores and the inhabitants reacted by departing their homeland by the tens of thousands. In the thirty years prior to 1960 only 30,340 Portuguese migrated to the United States, an average of about 1,000 per year. The annual average of new Portuguese immigrants arriving during the 1960s was higher than the total for the entire decade of the 1940s. In the thirty years between 1961 and 1990, the number of new Portuguese immigrants mushroomed to 226,810—a full 44.5 percent of the total Portuguese immigration to the United States since 1820—almost as many as arrived during the thirty years from 1890-1920, when worldwide immigration was at its peak[14] (see Figure 4).

FIGURE 4

PORTUGUESE IMMIGRATION TO THE UNITED STATES, 1820-1990

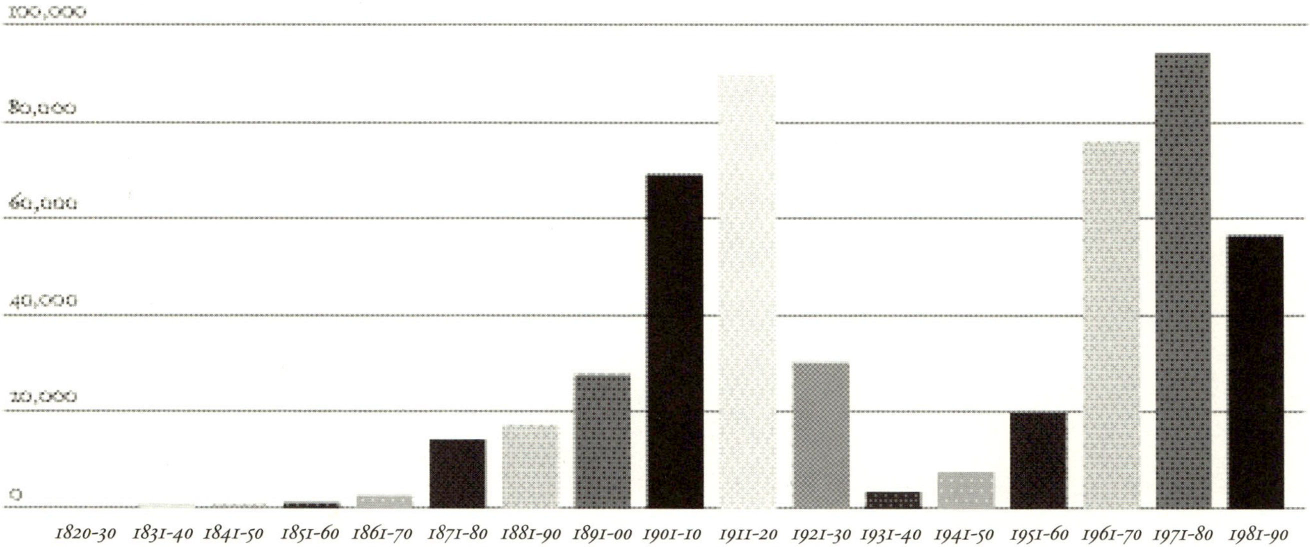
100,000
80,000
60,000
40,000
20,000
0
1820-30
1831-40
1841-50
1851-60
1861-70
1871-80
1881-90
1891-00
1901-10
1911-20
1921-30
1931-40
1941-50
1951-60
1961-70
1971-80
1981-90

Number	180	829	550	1,055	2,658	14,082	16,978	27,508	69,149	89,732	29,994	3,329	7,423	19,588	76,065	94,246	56,499	509,865

5,272–1%   247,443–48.5%   30,340–6%   226,810–44.5%

SOURCES: Immigration Naturalization Service 1976, Annual Report 86-88.
United States Census, 1990 (Portuguese primary ancestors).

The Portuguese immigrants of the last four decades of the 20th century were motivated by the same forces that compelled their compatriots to depart the Azores throughout the previous 150 years—namely, a chance to improve themselves economically. The ever-present specters of overpopulation and military conscription for the males, as always, were contributing factors. Little had changed in the daily life of Azoreans during the previous century-and-a-half. Immigrants now made the trip from the islands to the United States by jet but, for the majority, the four-hour flight was their first experience in an airplane.

Two characteristics of this third wave of immigrants, however, distinguish them from the earlier groups: education and a sense of nationality. Overall, they tended to be better educated than previous Portuguese immigrants. For most, the change was minimal, an elementary education for them versus no education for their grandparents and many of their parents. While their forefathers frequently thought of themselves as being from a particular village or island first, followed by the Azores and, lastly, as Portuguese, the new perspective was almost the reverse. A sense of being Portuguese permeated these newcomers. Granted, they were Azoreans from Pico, Faial, São Miguel or one of the other six islands, but they were Portuguese first. This sense of nationalism is a fairly recent phenomenon and a result, in part, of the nature of the prolonged colonial wars in Africa and the Portuguese government's efforts to generate patriotic support for an unpopular war.

The physical separation between the Azores and mainland Portugal is frequently reflected in delays, sometimes lengthy, between the arrival of a new idea or practice on the mainland and its appearance in the Azores. The islands are not, however, a static society—change does come. The people emigrating from these islands in the last third of the 20th century were proof that change was occurring in the homeland. They were noticeably different in their educational level, their sense of nationality, and an overall sense of being more aware of worldly events than their predecessors.

One area that had not changed was the importance of family and the reliance upon social networks to facilitate the migration process. Chain migration was still alive and well and the extensive social network between Portuguese in the United States and the Azores, which facilitated the finding of jobs and housing for newcomers, continued to encourage a high degree of concentration of Portuguese immigrants in a relatively small number of communities. Large numbers of immigrants, all in need of jobs, housing and other assistance, arrived in such a short period of time that they were inevitably a disrupting force, even if only temporarily. The enormous task of spatially and temporally accommodating the influx of new immigrants created adjustment problems for both new immigrants and established Portuguese-Americans.

Although the same single-minded focus on achieving economic well-being was as characteristic of past generations of immigrants as it was for the more recent arrivals, it caused disdain on the part of many Portuguese-Americans and non-Portuguese. In the generation between the second and third stage of Portuguese migration, major social legislation had been enacted to provide at least minimal economic security for the working population and the elderly in this country. In spite of the on-going concern about how to continue financing that legislation, it had generated major social changes. Children of immigrants, who themselves grew up in America, sometimes cannot fully appreciate the uncertainty and closed nature of the social and economic system left behind by their parents and, even less so, by the more recent immigrants from the Azores. Never having lived under such a system, nor having experienced the emotional impact of being an immigrant, second and third-generation Portuguese-Americans frequently cannot comprehend the immigrants' overriding concern with economic security. Most people went into debt to emigrate and the level of indebtedness usually increased while they were getting established in their new homeland. Before they could even start to think about achieving the economic security that motivated them to migrate in the first place, they had to turn their full attention to retiring those family debts. Usually, "every able-bodied member of a family contributes to its income and welfare."[15]

While they genuinely want to see these latest immigrants succeed, many Portuguese-Americans resented the plethora of government programs which, although designed to help immigrants adjust to their new environment, seemed to favor immigrants over native-born Americans. As one second-generation Portuguese-American expressed it in the late 1970s,

Sure! We came when you didn't have all this and that free money for immigrants and minorities. We had to work for everything we got.

Nobody gave us anything for nothing. Now these people are coming in and get bussed to special bilingual schools—so they don't learn English and are proud of it! They get free lunches, they get paid to go to school, they get everything free we had to work for. They buy 10 houses where we're lucky if we own one with the mortgage paid. And then you tell us we should be like them—pushy, grabby, and not even trying to be American! That's the thanks we get for working hard and keeping things right.[16]

Emigration to Canada

The Portuguese population of Canada was less than 4,000 individuals in 1953 when the Canadian Government, in an effort to promote economic development, revised its immigration laws and allowed the first boatload of Portuguese immigrants to enter that country. Most of those early immigrants went to work as agricultural laborers or unskilled construction workers for the railroads. The favorable response of the Portuguese to the opportunity to emigrate to Canada soon prompted the Government to increase its original quota of 500 per year.[17] In 1960, there were 22,434 Portuguese immigrants in Canada; ten years later the total reached 84,968;[18] and between 1971 and 1977 another 65,180 Portuguese immigrants arrived in Canada, with 16,333 arriving in 1974 alone.[19]

Even so, the Canadian government's figures are conservative and do not include the illegal Portuguese immigrants living in Canada. One study estimated the Portuguese population of Canada to be 220,000 in 1976 and noted the significant illegal immigration to Canada. Travel agents in both Portugal and Canada played significant roles in coaching prospective immigrants, for a fee, on how to come to that country on a tourist visa and then remain there illegally.[20] While there may be some question about the immigration process, the 1996 Census of Canada enumerated 335,110 Portuguese living in that country. Virtually all of them had arrived since 1953![21] The Portuguese migration to Canada is clearly substantial in number and recent in origin.

In many ways, the Portuguese immigration experience in Canada was almost a duplicate of what occurred in the United States. This was particularly true with regard to areas of origin, degree of settlement concentration, occupation, and the influence of social ties in determining who would immigrate, where they would end up and what they would do when they got there. About seventy percent of the immigrants were from the Azores and, in contrast to the early arrivals who started out working on farms or for the railroads, the vast majority of them ended up in the city. The city, in this case, was most often Toronto, which by 1980 had a Portuguese community of about 100,000.[22] Second only to Toronto was Montreal with a Portuguese community in excess of 20,000.[23] In 1980, ninety-four percent of all the Portuguese immigrants in Canada were concentrated in three provinces: Ontario, with seventy percent; Quebec, sixteen percent; and British Columbia, eight percent.[24]

Most of the male immigrants found unskilled jobs as construction workers, custodians in public buildings, or gardeners, while many of the women were employed as domestics or worked in the textile and clothing industries in Toronto.[25] A study of Portuguese immigrants in Toronto found that the decision to go to Toronto was strongly influenced, for the most part, by their contacts with other Portuguese immigrants already living there. Most immigrants either found jobs through their contacts in Toronto or relied heavily upon them for information about job opportunities. The kinds of jobs that were controlled by an immigrant's network strongly influenced long-term prospects of achieving job mobility or becoming trapped in a dead-end job.[26] Although Canada has tightened its immigration restrictions, it is still possible for an immigrant to sponsor other family members to Canada. These chain migrations influenced what area of Portugal the immigrants came from, maintained the flow of new arrivals, and ensured the new immigrants a place to stay and assistance in finding employment.

Culturally, the experience of the Portuguese immigrant in Canada is also similar to that in the United States. Even though they tend to congregate in cultural enclaves in Toronto and Montreal, most of the immigrants are forced to learn some English on their job and adapt to the Canadian way of doing things. Again, however, it is the children who most quickly learn English and, in spite of the admonitions of their parents, become Canadianized. The dream of migrating to Canada, working for a few years and then returning to the homeland recedes farther into the distance as the children grow up relating less to the old country than to the new one and unwilling to return to a land that becomes more foreign to them with each passing year.[27]

Ethnic Revitalization

Whatever the reaction to the sometimes over-zealous efforts of the
newer immigrants, which frequently got them stereotyped as "material-
istic greenhorns," the more recent wave of immigration prompted many
Portuguese-Americans to reconsider their cultural heritage. Whether it
derived from a desire to counter the negative image of Portugal and
Portuguese that some felt the more recent immigrants were creating, or
from a need to identify themselves as Portuguese as a means of distin-
guishing themselves from other ethnic groups, Portuguese communities
in the United States experienced an ethnic revitalization movement during the last quarter of the 20th century. Such movements were most
noticeable in urban areas, such as Fall River, New Bedford, Providence
and San Leandro, where many of the more recent immigrants are also
concentrated. Being "ethnic" no longer carried the stigma that it had
during the 1940s and 50s and, in fact, was increasingly viewed as a positive side of the American character. One of the most glaring inconsis-
tencies in the Portuguese ethnic revitalization movement, however, is
the attempt to identify with a classical, elitist culture characteristic of
mainland Portugal. This is a culture far removed from the peasant society of the Azores from which most first and second wave Portuguese
American immigrants originated.[28]

The evolving sense of ethnicity, in a positive sense, brought about
change in the United States as well. Political pressure resulted in the U.S.
Census Bureau modifying their criteria for determining ethnic heritage
of U.S. citizens in the Census of 1980. No longer was "ethnicity" based
solely on the country of birth of parents and grandparents. In its place
came a self-identification process and people who identified strongly
with multiple ancestry were able to declare a "primary ancestry" and
even "secondary ancestry." The inherent question "Who am I?" which
such self-identification promoted, enhanced a growing sense of ethnic
awareness in the country. Making changes in the type of information
collected in the census raised questions about the comparability of the
new data with more traditional ethnic information. For Portuguese-
Americans, and undoubtedly for other ethnic groups as well, people's
perception of who they are, ethnically speaking, still matched up well
with earlier ethnic categorizations of the country's population.

Settlement patterns, based on self-identification of being primarily of Portuguese ancestry used in the more recent censuses, continued to reflect historical patterns that were established in the 19th century and have been maintained, with relatively minor modifications down to the present.

Settlement Trends—1960-1990

As the Census of 1960 revealed, the continuing trickle of immigration and the first group of refugees were almost sufficient to maintain the population of Portuguese "foreign stock" in the United States at the 1930 level. The Census enumerated 277,402 residents with a Portuguese heritage in 1960, which was a drop of only 1,324 from the 1930 count (see Figure 3). Nationwide the distribution was a continuation of earlier patterns of concentrated settlement. Three states—California, Massachusetts, and Rhode Island—still accounted for eighty percent of the Portuguese "foreign stock" and an additional four states—Connecticut, Hawaii, New York, and New Jersey—none with as much as five percent, brought the combined total to 94.3 percent. Although Hawaii's Portuguese population continued its downward spiral, Connecticut, New York, and New Jersey all experienced noticeable growth (see Figure 3).

119

The U.S. Census of 1990 enumerated 900,060 people who declared that Portuguese was their primary ancestry. Since the Census of 1870, California and Massachusetts have each claimed to be home to about one-third of the total Portuguese population of this nation, and the distinction of which state had the largest population has switched back and forth several times in the past century-and-a-half. In 1990, California was again in first place with 30.6 percent of the total self-identified ethnic Portuguese. Massachusetts, with 26.8 percent of the national total was in second place. The other states that have also traditionally been home to a significant portion of the Portuguese in this country continued in that role: Rhode Island contained 8.5 percent, Connecticut 3.9 percent and Hawaii 4.4 percent. In 1990, these five states, the traditional U. S. homelands of Portuguese-Americans, continued to represent 74.2 percent of the nation's total. The spread of Portuguese into neighboring New Jersey and New York, which was clearly evident in the 1960 Census data, was even more apparent in 1990 when together they accounted for 10.7 percent of the total population (see Figure 3).

Portuguese Women Assembly Workers,
New Bedford, MA, 1969.
Spinner Publications, Inc.

Joseph D. Thomas. Portuguese Immigrant Family,
New Bedford, 1980. Spinner Publications, Inc.

Sausage factory, no date. Spinner Publications, Inc.

The East Coast

Within the states with large concentrations of people of Portuguese ancestry, the internal distributions have followed their historical pattern. The Portuguese "foreign stock" in Massachusetts in 1960, 95,324 individuals, was concentrated in the same six counties where the 1930 population of 105,076 was located. In spite of the approximate ten percent decline in the Portuguese population during those thirty years, there was only a slight decline in the percentage of concentration in those six countries from ninety-five percent to 93.1 percent. In 1990, 241,173 people in the state of Massachusetts declared themselves to be of Portuguese primary ancestry. That constituted twentieth-seven percent of all the Portuguese primary ancestry inhabitants in the entire United States of America. In 1990, those same six counties, where the Portuguese had been concentrated in 1930 and 1960, still accounted for 90 percent of the Portuguese population of the state (see Map 8).

The war effort of the 1940s provided a temporary reprieve for the depressed textile industry of Massachusetts and neighboring states, but the prosperity was short lived. The obsolete factories were unable to compete successfully in the economy of the 1950s and 1960s. As they closed down, unemployment became a serious problem in the former textile centers. Bristol County suffered from high unemployment rates throughout the 1960s and 1970s and was considered an economically depressed area.[29] The lack of jobs for long-time residents of Bristol County was compounded by competition from large numbers of unskilled Portuguese immigrants who arrived in the late 1960s and throughout the 1970s. Their arrival aggravated tensions in the already severely depressed communities where they concentrated. Even so, sixty percent of the Portuguese population of Massachusetts were still living in Bristol County in 1990. With only minor variations, the Portuguese settlement patterns in Massachusetts in 1990 were a mirror image of those of 1960.

There was little noticeable change in either the size or distribution of the Portuguese population in Rhode Island between 1930 and 1960. Each census found slightly more than 29,000 Portuguese "foreign stock" living in the state with ninety-nine percent of them located in the same four counties. In 1990, the 76,773 people in Rhode Island who declared Portuguese as their primary ancestry represented 8.5 per-

MAP 8

PORTUGUESE POPULATION OF MASSACHUSETTS, 1960

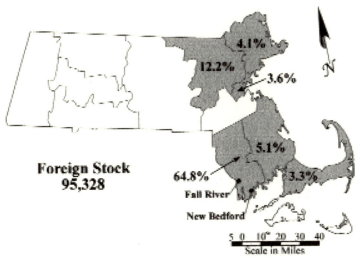

Foreign Stock
95,328

4.1%

12.2%

3.6%

5.1%

64.8%

3.3%

Fall River

New Bedford

5 0 10 20 30 40
Scale in Miles

Source: Census of the Population, 1960, Vol. I, Characteristics of the Population, Part 23, Massachusetts.

PORTUGUESE POPULATION OF MASSACHUSETTS, 1990

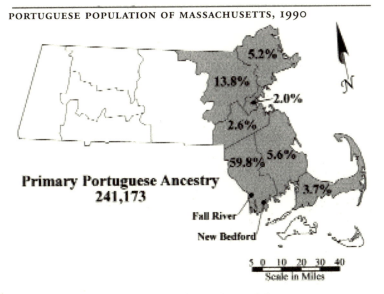

Primary Portuguese Ancestry
241,173

5.2%

13.8%

2.0%

2.6%

59.8% 5.6%

3.7%

Fall River

New Bedford

5 0 10 20 30 40
Scale in Miles

Source: United States Census, 1990

MAP 9

PORTUGUESE POPULATION OF CONNECTICUT & RHODE ISLAND, 1960

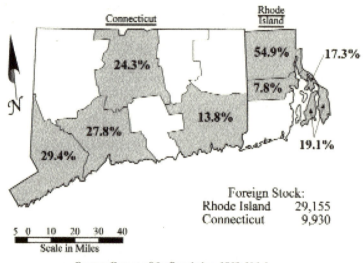

Source: Census of the Population, 1960, Vol. 1,
Characteristics of the Population, Part 8 & 41.

PORTUGUESE POPULATION OF CONNECTICUT & RHODE ISLAND, 1990

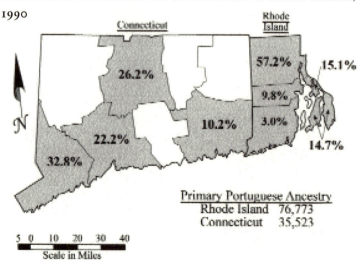

Source: United States Census, 1990.

cent of the nation's total Portuguese population—a two percent decline since the 1960 Census. Again, with only minor variations, the four counties that accounted for ninety-nine percent of the Portuguese living in the state in 1960 still was home to ninety-seven percent of the Portuguese in 1990 (see Map 9).

The Portuguese population of Connecticut doubled between 1930 and 1960 and, while they continued to be concentrated in four counties, the relative degree of concentration followed the direction of change that first occurred between 1900 and 1930. The percentage of Portuguese living in New London County, the old whaling center, steadily declined as the other three counties increased. Although the Portuguese population of Connecticut was still relatively small in 1960, by 1990, with 35,523 people declaring Portuguese as their primary ancestry, it represented almost four percent of the national total. The changes in settlement patterns obvious in 1960 were even more apparent in 1990. Fairfield County, one of the four counties where the Portuguese were most concentrated and the closest county to New York City, exper-ienced the most significant increase in Portuguese population; thirty-three percent of all Portuguese in the state were located there (see Map 9).

California

The West Coast experience during the last three decades of the 20th century was somewhat different from that which occurred on the other side of the continent. The Portuguese population of California declined slightly between 1930 and 1960 and the most noticeable change was in the relative distribution of that population. Both Los Angeles and San Diego counties, in the southern part of the state, had less than two percent of the Portuguese population in 1930. By 1960, the former was home to 5.2 percent of the Portuguese in California and the latter accounted for 3.5 percent. The major concentrations, however, continued to be in the San Francisco Bay Area and the Central Valley (see Map 10).

By the 1960s, Portuguese-Americans living in California were, for the most part, "solidly 'middle' in status as well as class."[30] Declining interest in their cultural heritage frequently accompanied Portuguese urban middle-class status. The Portuguese celebration in San Diego, for

MAP 10

PORTUGUESE POPULATION IN CALIFORNIA, 1960

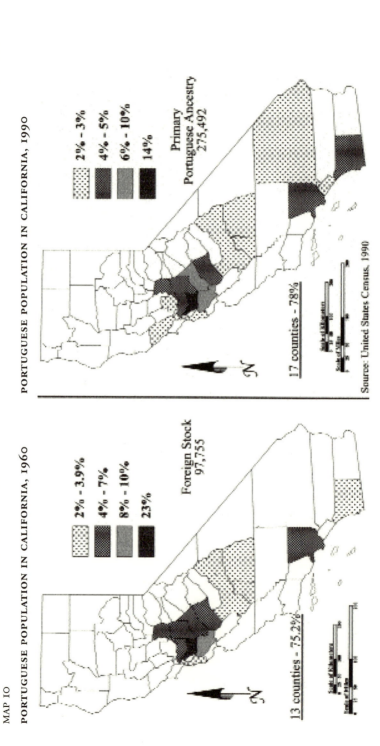

PORTUGUESE POPULATION IN CALIFORNIA, 1990

2% - 3%
4% - 5%
6% - 10%
14%

Primary
Portuguese Ancestry
275,492

17 counties - 78%

Source: United States Census, 1990

2% - 3.9%
4% - 7%
8% - 10%
23%

Foreign Stock
97,755

13 counties - 75.2%

example, died out in 1963 after being an annual event for more than fifty years. As one of its lifelong sponsors lamented: "Nobody wants to work on the *festas* anymore, we learned. The young people don't care. The old ones are dying out, getting too old for the responsibility."[31] In contrast to the East Coast, California attracted less than its "normal" share of new Portuguese immigrants arriving after 1965 and, consequently, Portuguese communities suffered from a lack of cultural revitalization. The 1990 Census enumerated 275,492 people in California who declared Portuguese to be their primary ancestry. Those 275,492 people represented thirty percent of the total Portuguese population of the nation—a five percent decline since the 1960 Census. In addition to the relative decline in California's percentage of the country's Portuguese population, there was a decided increase in the percentage living in urbanized areas of the state.

Although social networks continued to play a major role in determining the destination of new immigrants, economic opportunities for Portuguese immigrants in traditional California occupations had declined dramatically. With the changing nature of agriculture throughout the United States, particularly in the degree of mechanization, the increase in the size of the farms and, most importantly, the amount of capital required to enter farming, it was much more difficult for an immigrant to get started in farming in the 1970s than it had previously been. The small family farm was no longer a viable economic enterprise in California, and the would-be farmer was faced with the choice of getting bigger or getting out. In essence, working with or for a relative on a California farm was no longer a viable option for most immigrants. Unwilling or unable to remain on the farms where they were raised, many second and third-generation Portuguese-Americans joined the ranks of urban America during the 1970s. The likelihood that a newly-arrived immigrant could find a job in a factory or a service-related job on the East Coast was much greater than the prospect of ever becoming an independent farmer in California.

Although California is divided into fifty-eight counties, seventy-eight percent of the Portuguese population in 1990 was concentrated in three general groupings spread over seventeen counties. The largest concentration continued to be in the greater San Francisco Bay Area with twenty-four percent, with one in four of all California Portuguese living in Alameda and Santa Clara counties. When the other four Bay Area counties with a substantial Portuguese population were included, the number increased to thirty-five percent—one in three! Seven counties in the heart of the Central Valley of California, where agriculture has long been the primary focus, made up the second concentration. With Stanislaus County at the center, Sacramento County in the north and Kings and Tulare counties in the south, this grouping of agricultural counties housed twenty-nine percent of California's Portuguese in 1990. Southern California, with its large urban centers, was the location of the third general concentration of Portuguese. Los Angeles and San Diego counties, each represented about five percent of the total and Orange and San Bernardino counties each had slightly more than two percent—for a combined total of fourteen percent. California agriculture in general and the dairy industry in particular, continued to attract immigrants long after the population of the East Coast of the United States had made the transition from a rural to an urban-oriented society. By 1990 that attraction had ended.

Hawaii

Distance and discrimination combined to limit the Hawaiian Islands' attractiveness as a destination for Portuguese immigrants since the first importation of Portuguese families as contract laborers in 1878. The technology of modern transportation greatly reduced the time involved in getting from the Azores to the Hawaiian Islands, but at a substantial increase in price. One indication that the Portuguese-American population of Hawaii had finally overcome the economic liabilities that caused them to be discriminated against by the ruling Caucasian class was the emergence of a Portuguese cultural revival in the mid-1950s. One hundred years after they first began to immigrate to the Hawaiian Islands, there were indications that "many of Hawaii's Portuguese have become confident enough of their social and economic status to proceed beyond assimilation and to begin a search for their identity as a distinct and valued cultural group."[32]

Between 1930 and 1960, the Portuguese "foreign stock" in Hawaii declined from 15,408 to 9,325. After 1930, the Portuguese population of Hawaii had moved away from the agricultural islands and to the

MAP II

PORTUGUESE POPULATION OF HAWAII, 1960

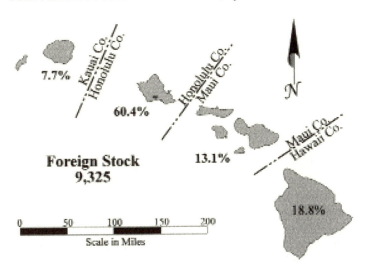

Foreign Stock
9,325

7.7%

60.4%

13.1%

18.8%

0   50   100   150   200
Scale in Miles

133

Source: Census of the Population, 1960, Vol. 1 Characteristics
of the Population, Part 13, Hawaii

PORTUGUESE POPULATION OF HAWAII, 1990

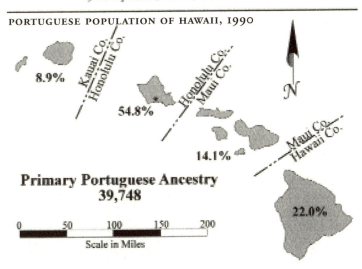

Primary Portuguese Ancestry
39,748

8.9%

54.8%

14.1%

22.0%

0   50   100   150   200
Scale in Miles

Source: United States Census, 1990

urban area of Honolulu. By 1960, 60.4 percent of the Portuguese population of Hawaii was located in Honolulu County. In the 1990 Census, 39,748 Hawaiians declared their primary ancestry to be Portuguese. The settlement pattern of Portuguese in Hawaii in 1990 was only slightly changed from that of 1960 (see Map 11).

New York & New Jersey

The largest concentration of Portuguese-Americans in the United States, employment opportunities and the ease of accessibility from the Azores at a relatively low price, attracted the majority of new Portuguese immigrants in the third wave of migration to the Eastern Seaboard. Fifty percent of the Portuguese primary ancestry population of the United States resided in the five states of Massachusetts, Rhode Island, Connecticut, New York, and New Jersey in 1990. Many of the former textile workers in Massachusetts, who were forced to leave that state when the textile industry collapsed in the 1920s and 1930s, settled in Newark, New Jersey, and found employment in the garment industry and other low-paying, non-skilled industries. These Portuguese immigrants, who were, for the most part, recent arrivals, formed the nucleus of a Portuguese community in New Jersey in Essex and Union counties. As recent newcomers, their social ties with friends and relatives still living in the Azores were very strong. When immigration restrictions were modified, first by the Azorean Refugee Acts and later by the revision of the basic immigration law in 1965, these former immigrants, now living in New Jersey, encouraged friends and relatives to join them. In 1990, when 56,928 residents declared Portuguese to be their primary ancestry, New Jersey was home to the third largest concentration of Portuguese on the East Coast[33] (see Figure 3). The neighboring state of New York, with its 34,455 primary ancestry Portuguese, represented 4.4 percent of the nation's total, primarily in Westchester, Queens and Nassau counties. Fairfield county in Connecticut, on the outskirts of New York City, is also an area of concentration.

*

Two major trends are apparent in the settlement patterns of Portuguese immigrants who arrived in the United States after the revision of immigration restrictions: a decided urban focus to their settlement patterns and the creation of a new East Coast core area of settlement surrounding New York City. One of the most obvious characteristics of the latest migration, both on the East and West Coast, is the inability of rural areas to attract new immigrants. Granted, the United States is an urban society, but the most persistent preservers of their Azorean cultural heritage have been those Portuguese living in rural areas. What the long-term impact of urban living in the United States will be on the perceived Portuguese ethnic heritage remains to be seen.

The emergence of a new core area of settlement illustrates, once again, the effectiveness of the social networks between Portuguese living in the United States and those remaining in the Azores. They continued to influence settlement patterns and provided employment opportunities for new immigrants, even though economic conditions changed radically since the 1920s when the second stage of migration was abruptly terminated. Neither agriculture in California nor textile mills in Massachusetts offered employment opportunities in sufficient numbers to accommodate the new influx of immigrants. There were still jobs, however, even for the unskilled, non-industrial immigrants from the Azores and particularly for those who were willing to take service jobs or industrial work at the lower entry levels. The urban focus of the current migration, with its emphasis on large urban centers such as Los Angeles, the San Francisco Bay Area, Toronto, Boston, Providence, and, increasingly, New York City, indicates that new arrivals are aware that the greatest availability of such jobs tends to be in or on the periphery of the larger urban centers. They are also quite willing to accept living in a large urban environment in order to have the opportunity to find what they seek most as immigrants—a chance to improve life materially for themselves and their families.

Notes

[1] S.L. Wolfbein, *The Decline of a Cotton Textile City: A Study of New Bedford,* (New York, 1944), *ii.*
[2] Ibid., 12.
[3] Ibid.,125.
[4] Ibid., 44.
[5] Ibid., 44.
[6] Ibid., 28-29.
[7] Ibid.,115-16.
[8] Leo Pap, *Portuguese American Speech: An Outline of Speech Conditions Among*

Portuguese Immigrants in New England and Elsewhere in the United States, (New York, 1949),14.

⁹ P.T. Silva, "The Position of 'New' Immigrants in the Fall River Textile Industry," *International Migration Review* 10 (2): 231-32.

¹⁰ Pap, *Portuguese American Speech,* 25.

¹¹ *Immigration and Naturalization Service, 1976 Annual Report,* (Washington, D.C., 1977), 86-88.

¹² Francis M. Rogers, "Americans of Portuguese Descent: A Lesson in Differentiation." *Sage Research Paper in the Social Sciences,* (Beverly Hills, 1974), 33.

¹³ Ibid., 33.

¹⁴ *Immigration and Naturalization Service, 1976 Annual Report,* 86-88.

¹⁵ Marilyn A. Trueblood, "The Melting Pot and Ethnic Revitalization" in *Ethnic Encounters.- Identities and Contexts.* G.L. Hicks and P.E. Leis. eds, (North Scituate, MA, 1977), 15. Also see, June Namias, "Antonio Cardoso-Boy from the Azores" in *First Generation: In the Words of Twentieth-Century American Immigrants,* (Boston, 1978), 171-75.

¹⁶ Estellie M. Smith, "Estão Aqui Mesmo," Unpublished paper, 11.

¹⁷ Caroline B. Brettell, "Ethnicity and Entrepreneurs: Portuguese Immigrants in A Canadian City" in *Ethnic Encounters: Identities and Contexts.* George L. Hicks and Phillip E. Leis, eds., (North Scituate, MA, 1977), 171.

¹⁸ Grace M. Anderson, *Networks of Contact: The Portuguese and Toronto,* (Waterloo, Ontario,1974), 9.

¹⁹ *Immigration Statistics Canada,* (Ottawa, Canada, various years 1971-1977).

²⁰ Grace M. Anderson and David Higgs, *A Future to Inherit: The Portuguese Communities of Canada,* (Toronto, 1976), 30-32.

²¹ Canada, Census of 1996.

²² Stanley Meisler, "Portuguese in Canada Cling to Old Ways," *Los Angeles Times,* Dec. 5, 1978, 20.

²³ Brettell, "Ethnicity and Entrepreneurs," 171.

²⁴ Anderson, *Networks of Contact,* 8.

²⁵ Brettell, "Ethnicity and Entrepreneurs," 172.

²⁶ Anderson, *Networks of Contact,* xiii-xiv.

²⁷ Meisler, "Portuguese in Canada Cling to Old Ways."

²⁸ Trueblood, "The Melting Pot and Ethnic Revitalization," 16.

²⁹ S. Wolforth, *The Portuguese in America,* (San Francisco, 1978), 61.

³⁰ H.H. Leder, "Cultural Persistence in a Portuguese American Community," (Ph.D. dissertation, Stanford University), 57.

³¹ L. Oliver, *Never Backward: The Autobiography of Lawrence Oliver—A Portuguese-American,* (San Diego, 1972), 148.

³² John Henry Felix and Peter F. Senecal, *The Portuguese in Hawaii,* (Honolulu, 1978), 119.

³³New Jersey is also the site of an extremely high concentration of newly-arrived immigrants from continental Portugal.

CHAPTER V

THE AZOREAN DILEMMA: TOO LITTLE FOR TOO MANY

Demographic Shifts in the Azores

The departure of thousands of emigrants from their homeland created a major demographic shift in the Azores. It provided, at least a temporary relief from too many people trying to eke out a living on too little land. In some cases, entire villages were depopulated and what had once been the case of an over abundance of labor became instead a shortage. By 1920, six of the Azores had had an obvious decline in population—Graciosa, São Jorge, Pico, Faial, Flores and Corvo had lost a total of 19,000 inhabitants, some twenty-two percent of their 1864 population.[1] In reality, however, the actual number of emigrants was equal to the apparent 19,000 loss plus the total natural increase in their combined populations.[2] What the natural increase in the population of that portion of the Azores was during those forty years is not certain; the best estimate is that it was somewhere between 20,000 and 42,000 people. What is certain is that by 1920, when the out-migration began to diminish as a result of restrictive legislation in the United States, the total loss through migration had resulted in a substantial reduction in the population density of those six islands. Faial went from 398 persons per square mile in 1864 to 286 in 1920, representing an average reduction of 112 persons per square mile! Flores' population density dropped almost seventy people per square mile, while Pico, Graciosa and São Jorge each declined by approximately fifty people per square mile in the same period.

The islands of Santa Maria, São Miguel and Terceira, on the other hand, together ended up with 17,883, or 11.4 percent more inhabitants in 1904 than in 1864. Due to the substantial out-migration during this time, this increase was substantially lower than would be expected through natural increase. Between 1904 and 1920, emigration increased rapidly and the population of the three islands declined by 10,452 people, an apparent six percent drop in population. When the natural increase is taken into account, the number of people who left during the sixteen years was at least double and probably triple the indicated apparent decline. However large the out-migration was from these islands, it was not sufficient to compensate for the natural increase in population. In 1920, the population density on São Miguel reached 388 persons per square mile—an increase of twenty-two people per square mile in the fifty-six years. On Santa Maria, the increase averaged sixteen per square mile during the same period. Terceira, somewhat more fortunate, lost virtually as many emigrants as it gained new population and was thereby almost able to maintain the *status quo*. In spite of the heavy out-migration that had taken place, what had been a difficult situation in 1864, with half of the population of the Azores crowded on these three islands, had, in fact, worsened by 1920.

Although out-migration substantially reduced population pressure on the limited resource base of the Azores, it was not accompanied by any change in the basic social, economic, or political structure of the islands. The overall situation in 1930 was little changed from the mid-1800s: it remained a traditional society interconnected through marriage and god-parentage ties; subsistence agriculture still dominated the economy; and, the government in Lisbon continued to treat the islands, politically and economically, as if they were a colony instead of an integral part of the nation. The general economic depression that beset the world during the 1930s virtually ensured that the nature of life in the islands, which had enabled the population to survive difficult times in the past, would remain unchanged. In effect, the "breathing room" which resulted from the reduced population pressure in the islands was not perceived as an opportunity to bring about needed structural changes, particularly in the economic realm where they were so badly needed. Given these conditions, it was inevitable that, in the absence of any significant out-migration, population pressure would begin to increase again and eventually reach crisis proportions.

One generation later, in the mid-1950s overpopulation was, once again, the over-riding problem in the Azores. In 1950, the population of the Azores had climbed to 316,287, an increase of 67,152 individuals in thirty years.³ The 1950 Census reveals a typical expanding population, with the largest number of people in the younger age groups and each cohort larger than the cohort born before (see Figure 5). In spite of the significant out-migration that had taken place prior to 1920, the 1950 age-sex pyramid does not have a noticeable gap in any particular cohort of the population, which illustrates the nature of that earlier migration. Migrations typically are selective, in that they attract primarily populations in the fifteen to forty-five age group, and their subsequent absence remains visible in an age-sex pyramid until the people in those age groups eventually cease to exist. The absence of any significant gaps in the 1950 age-sex pyramid illustrates the degree to which the previous migration was a chain migration of interrelated individuals which removed entire extended families—not just young adults—from the Azores.

139

The still-expanding population of the Azores attained an average density of 355 persons per square mile in 1950 and ranged from 570 persons per square mile on São Miguel (well above the 366 persons per square mile almost 100 years earlier) to 108 on Corvo. Even though it had the largest base population in 1920, São Miguel, through a combination of natural growth and intra-island migration, suffered from a disproportionate share of the inhabitants. Seventy-eight percent (52,422 individuals) of the total population increase in the archipelago was concentrated on São Miguel in 1950. In a subsistence-agrarian economy, high average population densities are a good indicator of a hand-to-mouth existence and such was certainly the case in the Azores by 1950. In relation to the amount of agricultural land on São Miguel, the actual density of the population exceeded 1,300 per square mile. Limited by the nature of their expanding population, future prospects for the Azoreans appeared rather bleak in 1950. Two unexpected events during the following decade offered a ray of hope in what was becoming a desperate situation: Canada gradually lowered its immigration barriers to selected countries, including Portugal; and a natural disaster, in the form of a volcanic eruption, persuaded the United States to admit Portuguese refugees.

Conditions in the Azores—The 1960s

The inhabitants of the Azores were in desperate straits by the mid-1960s and welcomed the relief promised by the new immigration laws. António

FIGURE 5

POPULATION PYRAMID OF THE AZORES, 1950

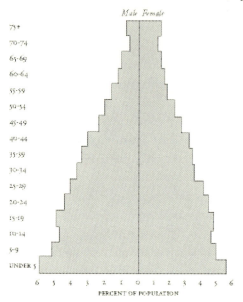

FIGURE 6

POPULATION PYRAMID OF THE AZORES, 1970

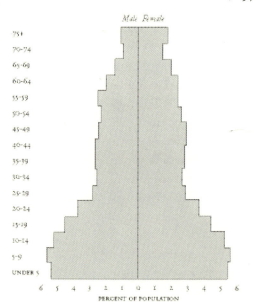

de Oliveira Salazar, the Portuguese dictator, had ruled that country with an iron hand since 1933 and few benefits trickled down to the Azorean Islands. In addition to the normal, heavy rate of taxation that Portuguese citizens endured, all goods imported to the Azores from a foreign country had to pass through Lisbon first, where a special tax was added. Any product being exported from the islands suffered the same fate. With little say in their local government and only token representation in the national government, the islands were, in every sense of the term, little more than a colony of mainland Portugal. Although they were officially recognized as an integral part of Portugal, they were never treated as such. In contrast to the situation in Portugal's African colonies, they were, however, Portuguese citizens and the traditional ties that had evolved over the past 400 years, partly a result of their proximity to the mainland, firmly identified them as Portuguese.

While most European colonial powers acknowledged changing world conditions in the post-World War II era and made plans to terminate, as gracefully as possible, the colonial status of their former territories in Africa, Portugal was determined to maintain control over its African colonies. Salazar reacted to African demands for independence by sending more troops to Mozambique, Angola and Portuguese Guinea, to which the Africans responded with the hit-and-run tactics of guerrilla warfare. For the next fourteen years a colonial war of attrition raged, with varying degrees of intensities, in Portugal's African colonies. Outnumbered almost two-to-one by its colonists, Portugal was hard-pressed to fight a three-front war. Once again, the young men of the Azores were faced with conscription into the Portuguese Army, but instead of being stationed on the mainland for several years, they now faced the probability of being sent to Africa to fight in a guerrilla war which they could not hope to win. Even Salazar's abdication of power in 1968, a result of poor health, did not end Portugal's involvement in the three-front colonial war. His successor was as committed as Salazar had been to preventing Angola, Mozambique and Portuguese Guinea from becoming independent nations. As the war continued year after year with no end in sight, immigration to the United States or Canada appealed to more and more young men as an attractive alternative to going off to fight in an unpopular war in Africa. Even parents with young children emigrated to avoid the prospects of future military service for their young sons.[4]

Milton Silvia. Plowing Fields, São Miguel, Azores, 1979.
Spinner Publications, Inc.

Milton Silvia. Chopping Brush. Faial, Azores, 1988.
Spinner Publications, Inc.

In spite of the number of Azoreans who immigrated to Canada or the United States during the last half of the 1950s, the population of the islands continued to increase and reached a new high of 327,421 individuals in 1960.[5] As the pressure on the limited amount of agricultural land intensified, the dichotomy inherent in the traditional system of land ownership became even more conspicuous. Of the 40,710 agricultural landholdings in the Azores in 1965, 81.8 percent were less than three hectares in size[6] and yet those 81.8 percent controlled only 33.7 percent of all agricultural land.[7] Their counterparts, the number of holdings in excess of ten hectares, which included only 3.2 percent of all the farms, accounted for 31.8 percent of the total agricultural land. On some islands the contrasts were even more extreme. On São Miguel, for example, 88.3 percent of the farms were concentrated on forty-six percent of the agricultural land on the one hand, while on the other, 27.2 percent of the land was controlled by only 2.1 percent of the farms. With only 38.0 percent of the land even marginally suitable for agriculture and the population still increasing, the prospects of the younger generation being able to acquire enough land to support themselves were very poor.

The possibilities for urban-oriented employment were not any better. With only slightly more than 21,000 inhabitants in 1970, Ponta Delgada, São Miguel, was the largest urban center in the Azores. It was followed by Angra do Heroismo, Terceira with 16,000 and Horta, Faial with 7,000 residents.[8] As district capitals, they were able to provide a limited amount of employment in the various government agencies, but even that was minimal. Lacking an industrial base and without any prospects of acquiring one, the three urban areas were limited to basic processing and packaging of agricultural products and providing goods and services for a poor, rural population. With the exception of the military base on Terceira, non-urban service employment was virtually nonexistent. The air base, which the United States leased from Portugal, provided employment for a number of Azoreans as support staff for the base and the American servicemen stationed there. However, the revenues from leasing the base went to the Portuguese government. Although they welcomed the employment that the installation provided, the natives of Terceira found themselves exposed to conspicuous consumption and forced to compete with the comparatively wealthy American servicemen for housing and other goods and services in the nearby villages. Although the "ugly American" syndrome contributed to a sense of resentment toward American servicemen, it also reinforced the myth that everyone in America was wealthy and helped entice young Azoreans to become immigrants.

Indications that a third wave of migration was in motion first became apparent in the 1960 Census when six of the nine islands registered an absolute decline in population.[9] Even though the other three islands also experienced out-migration after 1950, their net gain was sufficient to account for an overall increase in the archipelago's population between 1950 and 1960. The population of the Azores reached a new high of 327,421 in 1960 with an average density of 368 persons per square mile. Four of the nine islands exceeded 300 persons per square mile; São Miguel and Terceira, with 587 and 473 respectively, were at the top of the list.

149

The archaic land tenure system, which accentuated the perennial shortage of farmland, limited the ability of the agricultural sector to absorb an increasing population. The developing urban centers were equally unable to provide employment for the expanding labor force and, after 1960, the specter of compulsory military service to fight a colonial war in Africa weighed heavily upon the future of the young Portuguese population. With few prospects in their homeland, immigration was, once again, viewed as a viable alternative to a continually deteriorating economic and political situation. Fortunately, both Canada and the United States were receptive to receiving new immigrants in the 1960s and 1970s and many Azoreans took advantage of the opportunity and left the islands to join friends and relatives in America.

Emigration and Demographic Shifts

The 2001 Census of Portugal recorded a substantial drop in the Azorean population in the four decades following the 1960 Census; every island registered an absolute decline. The apparent loss of 85,348 inhabitants was, in fact, substantially higher; official emigration records indicate that 75,116 residents legally departed from the islands between 1960 and 1970 alone.[10] An age-sex pyramid of the 1970 population of the Azores clearly reveals which age group provided the bulk of the new migrants (see Figure 6). In 1970, the 20-45 age group accounted for only 14.5 percent of the males and 15.2 percent of the females, for a total of 29.7 percent; in 1950 the same age group contained 18.5 percent of the males and 18.6 percent of the females, or 37.1 percent of the total population (see Figure 5). The loss of young adults was also reflected in a decline in the number of births after 1965 and an increase in the proportion of the population over fifty. The impact of the new migration was primarily apparent in the absence of a substantial proportion of the young adult population. Once those new immigrants were firmly established in their new environment, the traditional chain migration broadened the effects of the out-migration on the remaining population as parents and siblings joined family members abroad.

The tide of Azorean emigrants ebbed and flowed from 1950 to 1990 in direct response to changes in immigration laws in the United States and Canada. During the first three years, before Canada opened its doors to new immigrants, the out-migration averaged only 750 per year; after Canada began accepting immigrants, the yearly average increased to 2,040 between 1953 and 1958. The impact of the Azorean Refugee Acts of 1958 and 1960 were reflected in a temporary increase to 6,800 in 1959 and 1960, afterwards the out-migration declined to 3,500 per year from 1961 until 1965 when most emigrants went to Canada. The revision in immigration quotas in the United States in 1965 prompted a substantial increase in emigration. During the following decade the annual flow of departees averaged 10,400.[11] In the twenty-five years prior to 1976, 146,899 Azoreans officially emigrated from their homeland.[12]

There was also a fairly substantial illegal immigration to both the United States and Canada throughout the remainder of the century. It was not uncommon for Portuguese citizens, and those from other countries as well, to visit the United States or Canada on a tourist visa, find a job through the efforts of friends or relatives, and simply neglect to return to their homeland. The Immigration and Naturalization Service did not check to see that tourists departed, and after several years the illegal immigrant could petition to have his or her status changed to that of a legal alien. Although it required obtaining legal advice to process the necessary papers, there was seldom any danger of being deported. Illegal immigration enabled the potential emigrants to leave their homeland immediately, once the decision was made to depart and avoid the delay of waiting one or more years for an opening in the annual quota of legal emigrants. It is impossible to determine precisely how many Portuguese availed themselves of this shortcut, but apparently many did.

Official emigration records indicate that fifty-three percent of the 38,150 emigrants who left the islands in the six-year period 1970-1975 were destined for the United States, while forty-five percent went to Canada. Only two percent of those who made the decision to leave the islands permanently chose a location other than the United States or Canada, which, again, illustrates the continuing influence of social ties in determining where an individual would go once the decision was made to emigrate. Although São Miguel accounted for fifty-two percent of the total Azorean population in 1970, it was the origin of only forty-one percent of the out-migration that occurred between 1970-1975. Apparently population pressures were perceived by the inhabitants as being more severe on the other islands than they were on São Miguel. The fact that Ponta Delgada, the largest urban center in the archipelago, was located on São Miguel and was able to offer a greater number of urban-oriented jobs may have also contributed to this perception. Of the 15,642 emigrants who left São Miguel during that time, fifty-eight percent were destined for Canada and thirty-nine percent for the United States. In contrast to São Miguel, sixty-one percent of those leaving Terceira ended up in the United States while only thirty-seven percent went to Canada.[13]

The dramatic decline in the population of the Azores between 1960 and 2001 demonstrated an increasing desire among the inhabitants of those picturesque islands for a better life and the opportunity, once again, to pursue that dream by emigrating to the United States or Canada. The extent of the out-migration that took place in this period was felt throughout the archipelago. In absolute numbers, the population dropped from 327,421 in 1960 to 242,073 in 2001. While the incentives to leave were obviously stronger on some islands than on others, overall average density dropped to 272 persons per square mile. The average decline in population for all the islands between 1960 and 2001 was twenty-six percent. The figures ranged from a high of fifty-eight and forty-five percent respectively, for the islands of Santa Maria and Graciosa, to a low of twenty-two percent for São Miguel.

Economic and Political Change

The size and nature of the population decline significantly reduced competition for employment among the younger generation of the island. The loss of so many inhabitants, even from what had become an over-populated environment, created problems of adjustment. During the summer of 1978, for example, common complaints heard in the islands were that it is almost impossible to get dependable agricultural workers and that the cost of labor had risen so much that a farmer could not afford to hire help. The decline in the large surplus population reduced competition for employment and, consequently, increased the cost of labor. One response to increased labor costs was apparent in changing land use patterns. Large areas, formerly devoted to intensive agriculture, were converted to pasture for beef cattle due to increased labor costs, the difficulty in obtaining adequate help, and the existence of a ready market for beef cattle in mainland Portugal. At the same time, to feed their population, the islanders were forced to import corn and other foodstuffs, which they had customarily produced. Other traditional labor-intensive activities also suffered from the changing labor market. Handcrafted artifacts, typical of the Azores, became difficult to find and, if available, were frequently produced in Madeira. Weaving, for local consumption or the occasional tourist, virtually disappeared from the islands.

Shore-whaling, introduced into the islands by American whalers in the 1850s, also disappeared. As late as 1954, it was noted that

> "[s]perm whaling in these islands is especially interesting because the methods employed are a survival of that old-time whaling generally believed to have quite vanished from the seas. Shore-whaling off the coasts of the Azores, prosecuted with the hand harpoon and lance from open boats under oars or sails, is still a considerable industry."[14]

Although a study of Azorean whaling in the late 1960s found it to still be a viable occupation on the islands of Pico and Faial, by 1978 it was being pursued by a dwindling number of aging, part-time whalers who primarily occupied themselves as longshoremen and farmers—even as they listened for the sound of the exploding rocket that traditionally called them to their boats. The whaling village of Lajes do Pico, home of one of the last shore-whaling crews in the Azores, in its own way, felt the impact of out-migration from the islands as sharply as the farmers on São Miguel and Terceira. Whaling, Azorean style, was a hazardous occupation with marginal rewards. As such, it rarely attracted young men who found it much easier and more rewarding to seek their fortunes in a foreign country than in a whaleboat and, like so many other traditional occupations once common to these islands, whaling disappeared from the shores of the Azores.

The out-migration that took place during the last thirty-five years of the 20th century sent shock waves throughout Azorean society. With modern transportation, the United States and Canada are now only a four-hour flight away from the Azores and the flow of traffic between these islands and those two countries is substantial. In time-honored tradition, many emigrants continued to send money to members of their family still living in the Azores, and return visits from fairly recent immigrants were not uncommon. Their accounts of jobs and living conditions in the new country continued to stimulate the flow of immigrants and were also partially responsible for a growing sense of dissatisfaction with life in the islands. Traditional occupations fell by the wayside as young people sought alternatives elsewhere and demands for more and improved services, which most saw as long overdue, became widespread.

The bloodless revolution of 1974 brought an end to Portugal's oppressive dictatorship and disastrous three-front African war. Democracy was established—the onerous secret police was dismantled, freedom of speech and of the press were instituted, and open elections were held. In the year following the revolution, independence was also granted to all of the African colonies. After four decades under Salazar's regime, it was, for most Portuguese, their first experience with democracy and a society in which they could express their political opinions. For many young men, it also meant freedom from conscription into the colonial wars. The social and economic problems in what was still a rather underdeveloped nation have, however, proved difficult to resolve, and poverty and very limited economic opportunity continued to be an intractable part of life on the mainland as well as in the Azores and Maderia. Migration thus remains an attractive option for Azoreans and the immigrant populations of both the United States and Canada have continued to grow throughout the 20th century.

Political and economic changes in Portugal enabled the country to qualify for membership in the European Community in 1986. As always, the question remains of how to deal with the two island regions that, territorially speaking, are considered to be an integral part of the nation. In the political restructuring of the country, the immediate solution was to create two autonomous regions—one for the Azores and the other for Madeira. Although the long-term strategic locations of these two autonomous island groups are important in the geo-political machinations of the western world, the short-term, day-to-day problems of life in these islands continue to suffer from benign neglect. Creating a progressive educational system and developing an economic infrastructure based on up-to-date transportation facilities, modern communications and power systems can best be described as aspirations yet unrealized. As always in the past, isolation from the mainland continues to be both a blessing and a curse for the Azores.

154

Notes

[1] The apparent change in population between 1864 and 1904 is based on the enumerated population living in the islands at the later date and does not reflect the actual number of people who emigrated because it does not include the natural increase in population which also occurred over those forty years. Although the data necessary to calculate the actual rate of population growth for this period is nonexistent, an analysis of the Censuses of 1864, 1904, 1911, and 1920 provide some insights into patterns of population growth within the islands as well as emigration trends in the Azores.

POPULATION OF THE AZORES 1864-1920

Islands	Population 1864	Population 1904	Apparent Change since 1864	Population 1920	Apparent Change since 1904	Population P/SQ/M 1920
Santa Maria	5,683	6,479	+10.5	6,457	-0.3	174
São Miguel	105,404	120,404	+14.2	111,745	-7.2	388
Terceira	45,781	48,098	+5.1	46,277	-3.8	302
Graciosa	8,962	8,079	-9.8	7,479	-7.4	311
São Jorge	17,998	14,390	-20.0	13,362	-7.1	145
Pico	27,721	22,926	-17.3	19,925	-13.1	118
Faial	26,259	19,075	-27.4	18,917	-0.8	286
Flores	10,259	7,527	-26.6	6,720	-10.7	122
Corvo	888	758	-14.2	661	-12.8	98
TOTAL	249,135	247,686	-0.6	231,543	-6.5	260

SOURCE: *População dos Açores.* (Açores: Departamento Regional de Estudos e Planeamento, 1975), 1.

[2] Based on the crude birth and death rates reported in that census, it is possible to calculate an average annual natural increase of 11.99 per 1,000 population, 1.19 percent per annum for the archipelago.

3

POPULATION OF THE AZORES 1920-1950

Islands	Population 1920[1]	Population P/S/M	Population 1950[2]	Apparent Change Since 1920	Population P/S/M 1950
Santa Maria	6,457	174	11,844	+5,387	320
São Miguel	111,745	388	164,167	+52,422	570
Terceira	46,277	302	60,372	+14,092	394
Graciosa	7,477	311	9,517	+2,040	396
São Jorge	13,362	145	15,529	+2,167	168
Pico	19,927	118	22,557	+2,630	134
Faial	18,917	286	23,923	+5,006	362
Flores	6,720	122	7,650	+930	139
Corvo	661	98	728	+67	108
TOTAL	231,543	260	316,287	+67,152	355

SOURCES:

[1] *Súmula de Dados Estatísticos,* (Açores: Departamento Regional de Estudos e Planeamento, 1976), 4.

[2] *População dos Açores,* (Açores: Departamento Regional de Estúdios e Planeamento, 1975).

155

[4] Information is from interviews conducted in the Azores by the author in the summer of 1978.

[5] *10° Recenseamento Geral da População no Continente e Ilhas Ajacentes, 1960,* Tomo 11, (Lisboa, 1960).

[6] A hectare of land is approximately 2.5 acres.

7

AGRICULTURAL LANDHOLDINGS IN THE AZORES 1965

Islands	Number of Holdings	Area in Farmland (Hectares)	0-3 Hectares (Percent)		3-5 Hectares (Percent)		5-10 Hectares (Percent)		More than 10 Hectares (Percent)	
			Farms	Area	Farms	Area	Farms	Area	Farms	Area
Santa Maria	1,754	2,857.35	87.0	47.9	7.8	18.4	3.9	16.9	1.3	16.8
São Miguel	17,494	30,854.80	88.3	46.0	6.0	12.9	3.6	13.9	2.1	27.2
Terceira	8,487	18,868.17	80.0	29.8	10.5	18.3	6.8	20.6	2.7	31.3
Graciosa	1,980	2,732.66	88.8	51.1	5.9	16.2	4.2	20.7	1.1	12.0
São Jorge	2,911	10,381.59	68.0	17.6	11.6	12.7	11.9	23.7	8.7	46.0
Pico	4,172	12,239.30	74.5	22.2	9.9	13.0	9.3	21.9	6.3	42.9
Faial	2,428	6,777.80	68.0	28.2	19.4	26.9	9.9	23.8	2.7	21.1
Flores	1,373	4,490.38	72.5	23.2	12.8	15.1	9.0	18.7	5.7	43.0
Corvo	111	375.97	48.7	23.7	31.5	35.4	17.1	32.1	2.7	8.3
TOTAL	40,710	89,578.02	81.8	33.7	8.9	15.6	6.1	18.9	3.2	31.8

SOURCE: *Súmula de Dados Estatísticos,* (Açores: Departamento Regional de Estudos e Planeamento, 1976), 21.

[8] *Açores: Do 25 de Abril até aos nossos dias.* (Lisboa, 1977), 143.

9

POPULATION OF THE AZORES 1960-2001

Islands	Population 1960	Apparent Change Since 1950	Population P/SQ/M (1960)	Population 2001	Apparent Change Since 1960	Population P/SQ/M (2001)
Santa Maria	13,180	+1,336	356	5,628	-7,552	152
São Miguel	169,170	+5,003	587	131,510	-37,660	456
Terceira	72,479	+12,107	473	55,794	-16,685	365
Graciosa	8,634	-883	362	4,770	-3,864	199
São Jorge	14,764	-765	160	9,681	-5,083	105
Pico	21,626	-931	128	14,804	-6,822	88
Faial	20,343	-3,580	308	15,476	-4,867	234
Flores	6,556	-1,094	119	3,992	-2,564	72
Corvo	669	-59	100	418	-251	62
TOTAL	327,421	+11,134	368	242,073	-85,348	272

SOURCES: *Recenseamento Geral da População do Continente e Ilhas Adjacentes,* em 15 de Dezembro 1960. Tomo II, Instituto Nacional de Estatística Lisboa, 1960. *XIV Recenseamento Geral da População,* Censos 2001.

[10] *Açores: Do 25 de Abril até aos nossos dias,* 144.

[11] Data provided by the Director of the Department of Emigration in Horta, Faial, during the summer of 1978.

[12] *Açores: Do 25 de Abril até aos nossos dias,* 144.

[13] Data provided by the Director of the Department of Emigration in Horta, Faial, during the summer of 1978.

[14] R. Clarke, "'Open Boat Whaling in the Azores' The History and Present Methods of a Relic Industry" *Discovery Reports* 26: 283. Stepping into an Azorean whaling boat was like taking a step backwards in time. The equipment and techniques employed by these 20th century hunters were identical to those used over one hundred years ago by American whaling vessels. Even the terminology employed in the hunt was retained and passed on from the earlier whaling period.

CHAPTER VI

ETHNIC SURVIVAL: THE MAINTENANCE OF CULTURAL VALUES

Azoreans, like all other people, are a product of their physical and cultural environments, and when they migrated to America their cultural heritage accompanied them. Given the close nature of their kinship ties and social interaction in their homeland, it was neither unexpected nor unusual that those networks of family and friendship would direct a chain migration of new immigrants to locations inhabited by fellow Portuguese. The human geography of Portuguese in America, as reflected in their settlement patterns, was a direct outgrowth of the triad of family, community and church that totally dominated and connected Azorean life. These concentrated settlement patterns reinforced the maintenance of a Portuguese cultural identity among new immigrants and subsequent generations through the retention of traditional cultural practices.

Fraternal Organizations

As an ethnic group, the Portuguese were never significant, in terms of absolute numbers, in the total population of the nation. In certain areas, however, on the East and West Coast of the United States they are quite important regionally and in fact are the dominant ethnic group in a number of communities. The concentration of Portuguese immigrants and their offspring in a relatively small number of locations facilitated the continued utilization of their native language, provided a pool of suitable marriage partners for young adults, and enabled their community to ignore the developing social services in this country and continue, in times of need, their own tradition of self-help. During the first stage of migration, when illness, an accident or death beset a Portuguese

157

Joseph D. Thomas. Costa's Fish Market, Fall River, MA, 1998.
Spinner Publications, Inc.

Mount Carmel Church, New Bedford, 1913.
Spinner Publications, Inc.

Holy Ghost Procession, no date.
Spinner Publications, Inc.

family, it was common to take up a collection in the community to
help those in need. Meager though such donations were, they generally
sufficed to bury the dead and provide temporary assistance to the living. A number of fraternal and mutual aid societies gradually evolved
out of these early efforts to help one another. One of the earliest was
the *Associação Portuguesa Protectora e Beneficente* (Portuguese Protective
and Benevolent Society), which was formed in San Francisco on July 6,
1868. Its primary function was "to protect the living and bury the
dead."[1] In addition to the mutual aid funds which went to the widow
and children of the deceased, these early fraternal societies dignified the
burial of the immigrant, usually with a simple ceremony at the ceme-
tery, and rendered aid and sympathy to the bereaved.[2] Branches of the
Portuguese Protective and Benevolent Society soon appeared in other
communities in the Bay Area. Hayward, for example, formed a branch
in March, 1870, while San Leandro's appeared in July of the same year.[3]

Initially, most of these fraternal and mutual aid societies, like the
União Portuguese do Estado da California (Portuguese Union of the State
of California), or U.P.E.C. as it was commonly known after its founding
in San Leandro in 1880, would assess their surviving members $1 each
upon notification of the death of a member. The size of the paying membership determined the amount that went to the deceased's family. The
variation in benefits and the cumbersome nature of the collection process
resulted in efforts to standardize both costs and benefits, and the societies
were gradually transformed into a system of regular insurance coverage.
By 1892, members of the U.P.E.C., for example, were paying regular
monthly dues which insured that, when they died, their beneficiary
would receive a set amount of money.[4] The benefits of belonging to such
an organization were readily apparent to all, and membership in the various societies flourished. Local branches of the fraternal organizations
appeared in Portuguese communities on both coasts of the United States
and by 1918, the U.P.E.C., which was just one of several Portuguese fraternal societies in California, had 12,491 paying members.[5]

Membership in the early fraternal societies was exclusively for males,
but in 1898 the *Sociedade Portuguesa Rainha Santa Isabel* (Portuguese
Society of Queen Saint Isabel) was formed as a women's society to serve
as a focal point for cultural and charitable activities among the
Portuguese. It also provided a standard insurance benefit for its mem-

164

bers. The number of chapters increased rapidly and the S.P.R.S.I. became the most prestigious Portuguese women's organization in the United States. As late as 1974, it still had 13,500 members.[6]

While the mutual aid benefits provided financial assistance to the survivors of deceased members, the living enjoyed the fraternal aspects of the societies. As the organizations became more formalized, local chapters held regular monthly business meetings, elected local officers, and selected delegates to attend the annual regional and statewide meetings. These local meetings, which were conducted in Portuguese, were as much social as business affairs and were instrumental in maintaining interaction within the Portuguese community. The annual meetings, which were filled with pomp and ceremony designed to instill a sense of pride in being Portuguese, were occasions for the immigrant population to reaffirm ties with friends and relatives living in other communities and for their children to associate with other young Portuguese people.

While the meetings and social activities of the fraternal societies were instrumental in reinforcing the cultural values of the community and the use of the Portuguese language outside of the home, they also performed another important function. "It was the various societies, with their rituals and social activities that often added color and ceremony to break the monotonous pattern of daily life and enriched the social life of the individual and the family."[7] Such "color" and enrichments were noticeably absent from the lives of most immigrants in the United States in the early 1900s. The difficult times that the Manuel A. family of California experienced in the 1920s and 1930s were shared by their urban counterparts working in the mills and sweatshops of New England. If anything, conditions were even worse for the city dwellers who were completely dependent upon earning an income to provide for their family. Rural inhabitants could at least grow part of their own food supply when jobs in New England mill towns became noticeably scarce after the mid-1920s.

The Catholic Church

The immigrant's life was a radical departure from the traditional lifestyle of the Azores. Invariably, everything seemed to be done differently in America and immigrants had little choice but to adapt. In the process of changing and making innumerable adjustments to life in this new world, many traditional practices were quietly abandoned by the wayside. In the midst of all the turmoil and uncertainty, however, the Church stood constant and unchanging and provided a welcome sense of security. A shared faith in the Roman Catholic Church was the most basic component of the Portuguese cultural heritage and the one most resistant to change. Immigrants and their children might give up their native language, anglicize their family name, and divorce themselves of everything that identified them as Portuguese, but they rarely gave up their religion. For the vast majority, it was a religion based on simple faith. Uneducated, they were not versed in the doctrine of the Church but rather in the ritual. From their perspective, it was not necessary to understand the tenets of the Church as long as one had faith and followed the religious dictates of the priest. Bordering on mysticism, their religion combined an inordinate faith in the power of saints with a strict devotion to the ritual and ceremony of the mass.

Millions of other immigrants were also adherents of the Catholic faith, particularly those from southern Europe, and the Church was already well-established in America when most of the Portuguese arrived. Regional variations exist in all institutions, even in those religious institutions professing the same basic doctrines, and the Portuguese preferred their churches in America to be similar, both in ritual and appearance, to the ones they left behind in the Azores. A Portuguese priest was first sent to New Bedford in 1867 to care for the religious needs of the Portuguese immigrants concentrated there[8] and when sizeable Portuguese communities became established in other cities, such as Fall River, Providence, and San Leandro, they continued the practice of seeking priests who were familiar with their cultural heritage and could speak their native language. Although the total number of Portuguese-speaking priests was never very large, the concentrated settlement patterns of Portuguese immigrants made it possible for a limited number of priests to maintain contact with a substantial body of immigrants. Outlying communities that were unable to support a Portuguese priest of their own had to be satisfied with a visiting Portuguese priest, who came from the nearby cities, to say the mass for the local *festa* and for other special occasions.

In addition to a preference for Portuguese-speaking priests, many of the Catholic churches built in Portuguese communities were modeled after churches in their homeland. The architecture often brought back memories of the old village churches and the interior always contained the familiar symbols, particularly the images of the saints, so associated with their religion in the Azores. When all else failed, the Church remained the one continuous link with the past and "strove to remind the immigrant of his faith and struggled to keep the faith alive in the face of countless obstacles."[9]

Closely related to the Church is the system of godparentage that is itself a fundamental institution in the Portuguese community. At the time of baptism, every infant needs a godmother and a godfather to serve as sponsors. Traditionally, parents invited a brother, sister or a very close friend to be godparents to their children. While the primary function was to ensure the religious training of the child, becoming a godparent also established a special relationship, not just between the godparents and the child, but with the child's natural parents as well. In traditional Portuguese society, an intricate system of community ties and relationships, only marginally related to the Church, evolved from the religious need for godparents. These relationships were based on mutual obligations, responsibilities, and rights and further strengthened and expanded the normal family bonds. In times of crisis an individual's *compadres*, the godparents of his children and the parents of his godchildren, could always be relied upon for comfort and assistance. They also joined in and helped celebrate the more memorable occasions that occur in every family.

It was not uncommon for immigrants to have to borrow money to pay their passage to America and they frequently turned to parents, siblings and *compadres* for such assistance. After securing a job and a place to live, they saved their money, repaid the loan, and encouraged others to join them. Well aware of the meager existence that was the fate of most people in the Azores, they felt a strong sense of obligation to help those closest to them—brothers, sisters, parents and *compadres*. After a second member of the family emigrated and found work, they customarily pooled their resources to help those left behind come to the United States. In this way, entire extended families took part in chain migrations from their homeland to a particular community in this country. The ties that helped maintain traditional Azorean society—family, church, and community—were reinforced and transported with them,

167

but the role of the godparent, which combines both religious and family ties, suffered in the subsequent assimilation process. Although the special relationship between *compadres* and between godparents and godchildren remained intact for the immigrants and their children, its significance began to decline with the third generation and by the fourth generation being a godparent was little more than a religious ceremony.

Maintaining Cultural Traditions—Regional Variations

All Portuguese immigrants brought their cultural heritage with them to America, but the Portuguese in California were the most successful in retaining that heritage and passing it on to subsequent generations. Where the new immigrants settled and what occupations they ended up pursuing, which was largely determined by the social connections between prospective immigrants and those already in America, were the key factors that influenced the length of time that cultural traits were retained. It was only in California that a large number of Portuguese settled and remained on farms. Eighty-seven percent of all the Portuguese farm residents in the United States in 1960 were living in California, where the Portuguese have remained the most rural ethnic group in the state since the close of immigration in the early 1920s.[10] The predominantly rural nature of Portuguese settlement in California isolated the immigrants culturally as well as spatially and, as a consequence, minimized the contacts between Portuguese immigrants and the non-Portuguese members of the host society. The lack of day-to-day contact with people, other than one's own family, the need to be self-sufficient, the general unavailability of many amenities common in urban areas, and the general sense of isolation commonly associated with rural life in the first half of the 20th century were conditions conducive to the continuation of old-world traditions among Portuguese immigrants in California.

Almost the exact opposite occurred in the industrial centers in New England, "where Portuguese immigrants, were forced to go outside their group and domestic circle, to work in the factories in subordinate positions, thus having to learn some English or remain in low manual jobs where little or no communication was needed."[11] For reasons already noted, most of the Portuguese immigrants who settled on the

East Coast ended up working as semi-skilled or unskilled factory laborers in cities like Fall River and New Bedford, Massachusetts, and Providence, Rhode Island. In 1960, eighty-seven percent of the Portuguese in southeastern New England were city residents and only one percent were working as agriculturalists of any type.[12] This is not to say that the Portuguese immigrants in New England abandoned their cultural heritage when they stepped off the boat from the Azores. Nothing could be farther from the truth. What it does indicate, however, is that the cultural conflict, which inevitably results when members of different groups are forced into close juxtaposition, occurred on the East Coast long before it began to be obvious among second and third-generation Portuguese in California.

In Hawaii, the de-emphasis of the Portuguese cultural heritage was an almost immediate reaction among the immigrants themselves when they perceived that the visible signs of that heritage—*i.e.*, language, occupation and social practices—made them targets for discrimination. As early as 1941, it was noted that,

> there is a wide cultural differentiation between the Portuguese in the Island setting and those in California today. Although there have been changes in cultural patterns of the Portuguese in California, it is in Hawaii, where the Portuguese people have gone through the process of competition, conflict, accommodation, and assimilation and have broken down social distance, that the distinction from the old world pattern is most evident.[13]

The economic rewards associated with agriculture in California, where immigrants were drawn to the rural areas, were a marked contrast to the situation in Hawaii, where they fled from agriculture to the urban areas.

Local Festas

Summer was a great time to be Portuguese in California. A *festa*, or celebration, was held almost every weekend in some community in the Central Valley or along the coast and everyone looked forward to the occasion. It was a time for dancing, eating and socializing. Traditionally, every Portuguese community of any size would hold an annual Holy

Ghost celebration. Most of these were two-day affairs that began with a candlelight procession on Saturday night. The procession transported the queen's crown from the house of the sponsoring family to a chapel in or near the church. Afterwards, a dance was held in the local Portuguese Hall where the *chamarrita*, a traditional folk dance, shared the floor with less traditional dances. The following day a parade, complete with suitably-gowned outgoing and incoming queens, participants from fraternal organizations in all nearby towns, and statues of saints from the church, would transport the queen's crown from the chapel, through town, and end up at the church where the participants attended mass. At the conclusion of mass, the crown would be blessed, the new queen crowned and the procession would march back to the chapel. Afterwards a traditional meal of meat and bread was served free to the public.[14]

The local Portuguese celebration remained visible in California long after it ceased to exist in most New England and Hawaiian communities. It contributed to the maintenance of strong ties among the Portuguese population by facilitating the exchange of news and information among the members of a rural population and transmitting the cultural traditions of the immigrants to their children. The children were just as much a part of the festivities as adults. They learned to dance the *chamarita*, marched in the procession, and enjoyed the afternoon meal as much as their parents. In the process, they grew up accustomed to hearing Portuguese used as the common language not only at home but also at the social functions they attended. They also had ample opportunities to become acquainted with boys and girls who shared their cultural heritage. As one writer noted in 1941, "proud of their old-world background, their language, and their institutions, the Portuguese in California have sought to pass these things on to their children."[15]

In 1932, a group of Portuguese from Gustine, a small San Joaquin Valley town on the west side of Stanislaus County, in the Great Central Valley of California, decided to start a special celebration to attract Portuguese from all over California. They modeled their celebration on one that is held in the Azores, on the island of Terceira, and called it *Nossa Senhora dos Milagres* (Our Lady of Miracles). In contrast to the traditional two-day *festa*, the Gustine celebration quickly evolved into a full week of activities including : candlelight processions; nightly prayers at the Catholic church; the blessing of cows and distribution of milk and

Portuguese sweet bread; music and songs performed by Portuguese musicians; a Saturday night dance; an elaborate version of the traditional Sunday procession to and from the church; mass said by a visiting priest brought over from the Azores; an auction to raise money to help support the celebration; a carnival for children; a Sunday night dance; and, finally, on Monday, a bloodless bullfight copied after those held on the island of Terceira.[16]

While many of the local festas have atrophied and gradually disappeared, leaving behind only a somewhat dilapidated Portuguese Hall to vaguely remind third and fourth-generation Portuguese-Americans of their cultural heritage, the *festas* in the larger Portuguese communities in California are still commonplace. None, however, can compare to the Our Lady of Miracles celebration at Gustine. It has become a social event without par for the Portuguese population of California. In 1977, an estimated 28,000 people crowded into the small town of Gustine to help celebrate the annual Our Lady of Miracles festival. Forty-six Portuguese communities, some over 150 miles away, sent representatives, in the form of the queen of their celebration or members of their sponsoring fraternal organizations, to march in the parade on Sunday. Twenty decorated statues, the local queen and her attendants, all suitably gowned and robed, and six marching bands accompanied them. All in all it was a gala event which, though it cost in excess of $50,000 to stage, generated over $100,000 in revenues. The local Catholic Church, the thankful recipient of most of the profits from the festival, is prospering; the community is justifiably proud of its festival; Portuguese statewide took forward to the fall event; and the celebration continues to draw ever more participants each year.[17]

171

The East Coast counterpart of the Our Lady of Miracles festival is seen in the Blessing of the Fleet in Gloucester and Provincetown, the Feast of the Blessed Sacrament in New Bedford, and the Feast of the Holy Ghost in New Bedford and Fall River, all of which attract large enthusiastic crowds. It is primarily in California, though, that the rural-based Portuguese communities have continued to support their local as well as the more elaborate Our Lady of Miracles *festas*.

The survival of the *festa*, along with other cultural traditions, has been most tenuous in the Hawaiian Islands. Almost forty years ago it was noted that "Religious and fraternal festivals play a far greater part in the lives of California Portuguese than is the case with their brothers in Hawaii."[18] Their decline in Hawaii has become even more accentuated in the ensuing forty years.

Language

One of the earliest casualties of the acculturation process was the Portuguese language. It persisted the longest in large, urban Portuguese communities where many immigrants, particularly women not employed outside the home, were able to get by without learning English, and in the rural communities where there was little social or economic interaction with the English-speaking population. In the rural areas of California, for example, immigrants could get along quite well without learning English and, in fact, many of them never learned the language. At work and in the home, Portuguese was always spoken. On Sundays, the liturgy of the mass at the local Catholic Church was performed in Latin—as it had been in their homeland, and in some communities the sermon was delivered in Portuguese. The major social events, the summer *festas* in nearby towns, or the meetings of the fraternal organizations, were also occasions to converse in Portuguese. Although the children learned English in school, they were frequently informed that speaking English stopped at the outside door to the house.

The acculturation process weighed most heavily upon children of immigrant parents. Forced by law to attend school where their lessons and social interactions with non-Portuguese children were carried on in English, they learned to speak that language away from home while they continued to communicate with their parents in Portuguese. While many immigrants never learned English, their children became bilingual, at least to the degree of being able to function in either language. It was these children of immigrants, born in the United States and seldom formally taught Portuguese, "who were mainly responsible for the origin, use and propagation of anglicisms and for the deterioration of Portuguese in general.[19]

Changes in the Portuguese language in California took many forms, but primarily consisted of using an English word, with Portuguese pronunciation, to express a concept or object totally new to the immigrant; using an English word that sounded similar to a well-known Portuguese word, although with an entirely different meaning; and,

172

translating English into Portuguese literally on a word-for-word basis. The results frequently confus, amus or embarrass the Portuguese-speaking newcomer because the meaning in contemporary Portuguese is something quite different from that expressed in Californian Portuguese.[20] In spite of their linguistic deficiencies, second-generation Portuguese were quite capable of making themselves understood in either English or Portuguese and they continued the practice of speaking Portuguese whenever they were with other members of their own generation. They spoke it less frequently with their own children, however, who were rapidly being acculturated into the larger society.

The third generation became, for all practical purposes, unilingual, English-speaking Portuguese-Americans. Although they frequently understood some Portuguese, from hearing their parents and grandparents converse and from attending Portuguese celebrations, most were not able to communicate effectively in their grandparents' language.[21] On the East Coast of the United States, where urban living brought the immigrants and their children into daily contact with the English-speaking community, the process of learning English was frequently much more rapid. In the Hawaiian Islands, acculturation was even more accelerated than it was on the East Coast as the Portuguese hurried to disband as a nationality group.

173

Marriage

A more subtle way in which the passing years have eroded the Portuguese cultural traditions has been through the increasing incidence of out-marriage, .particularly among third and fourth-generation Portuguese-Americans. The habit of seeking marriage partners from their homeland, and frequently from their own village was common practice among first-generation Portuguese immigrants throughout the United States. The social interactions of the immigrants through their churches, fraternal organizations and celebrations ensured that most of the second generation found marriage partners within the Portuguese community. Again, the Hawaiian Islands were the main exception. In the late 1930s, 36.2 percent of the Portuguese males and 51.4 percent of the females were reported marrying outside their own ethnic group. In contrast, ten percent were estimated to be marrying outside their group in California at that time.[22]

It is among the third generation, and those that followed, that marrying non-Portuguese Americans has, understandably, become rather common. The third generation, typically, can neither speak nor understand Portuguese sufficiently well to be at ease in a Portuguese-speaking situation and are less likely to be actively involved in fraternal organizations, celebrations, and other social activities as their parents were as young adults. As a consequence, they are unlikely to interact socially with many suitable marriage partners who share their cultural heritage. Instead, most of their social activities, from the time they first enter the public school system, tend to be predominantly with English-speaking, non-Portuguese young people. By the time they are old

enough to start considering marriage, sharing a cultural heritage is not necessarily a high priority in choosing a partner. Those who marry outside the group were seldom active in the social activities of the Portuguese community before they wed and are less likely to be actively involved afterwards. The use of Portuguese at these activities, frequently not well understood by the Portuguese-American member and completely foreign to the non-Portuguese partner, makes it difficult for them to socialize. The offspring of such marriages generally do not learn much of their Portuguese heritage, do not learn the language, and are not active participants in the social activities of the group. In short, an almost complete breakdown occurs in the transmission of the traditional Portuguese culture to future generations.

Continuity and Change

Cultural values are not like an old pair of shoes that can be casually replaced when they are no longer in fashion. The cultural heritage which accompanied the Portuguese immigrants to America had provided the rationale for their very existence in the Azores and, as such, was not easily laid aside for the, as yet, untried traditions in this country. Those same traditions, which were so important to the immigrant, had less meaning, however, for each succeeding generation as they became more assimilated into the host society. While many of the more overt traditions—speaking Portuguese, active membership in fraternal societies, and participation in traditional celebrations—are not so common today among Portuguese-Americans, many of the basic values of

Portuguese society have remained. They still emphasize the importance of the family, the father continues to be the authority figure, and they strive to maintain their ties with the extended family. A study of cultural persistence among a Portuguese community in an urban setting in the early 1960s concluded that "while the Portuguese-American subculture has remained marginal, it has also maintained coherence, in contrast not only with most other American subcultures but also with the general culture of the 'receiving society.'"[23]

The Portuguese population of the United States has successfully maintained a strong sense of ethnic identity over an extended period of time. The nature of the migration process itself contributed to the maintenance of Portuguese communities and the general feeling of "being Portuguese." Instead of a single mass migration of immigrants who were then widely scattered throughout the country, Portuguese immigrants have continued to come to the same general locations since 1870. The traditional Portuguese cultural values were constantly reinforced by the arrival of new immigrants. In the absence of any new influx of Azorean immigrants, most visible signs of their culture might be expected to disappear gradually. The flow of immigrants was severely curtailed as a result of the restrictive legislation of the early 1920s when the Portuguese found, along with immigrants from all over the world, that the portals to America, although not completely closed, were greatly constricted. Since immigration to the United States opened up once again in the 1960s, a quarter of a million newly arrived Portuguese immigrants have joined those who came decades earlier. Portuguese cultural values, far from being an endangered species, are experiencing a revitalization as a result of the current migration. Those cultural values may not be exactly the same as they were in the 19th and early 20th centuries, but they certainly reflect a Portuguese cultural heritage.

*

The Portuguese migration from the Azores, and to a much lesser extent the mainland, to the United States during the past 180 years was neither unique nor unusual. At various times in their 400 year history, the inhabitants of these islands have been faced with serious overpopulation, declining agricultural productivity, and a variety of other natural and man-made disasters. They have reacted to these disasters as people the world over have reacted, by seeking alternatives elsewhere. By departing their native land, they have provided temporary solutions to the problems at hand for those who have remained behind. Lacking any substantial changes in the basic structure of the traditional agrarian economy of these islands, the problems that motivated a particular generation to leave periodically recur to haunt future generations. Given the reproductive capabilities of the human population and the seeming non-existence of economic alternatives in the Azores, the problems of the past seem ordained to reappear in the future. Whether the alternatives of the past will continue to be viable in the future is another question entirely. As the restrictive immigration legislation that was widely adopted in the 1920s illustrates, the potential immigrant today is very much at the mercy of the political whims of governments everywhere. Political boundaries can be readily manipulated in the 21st century—when it is to the advantage of the host society, they are permeable for selected immigrant populations. When conditions change, those same boundaries can, just as quickly, become impermeable. In the 21st century, migration on a large scale is no longer a realistic solution to humanity's problems. Without the possibility of large-scale migration, we may be forced, as human beings, to come to grips with the basic problems facing us in this century.

Notes

[1] August Mark Vaz, *The Portuguese in California,* (Oakland, 1965), 82.

[2] Ibid., 80.

[3] W. Halley, *The Centennial Year Book of Alameda County, California,* (Oakland, CA, 1876), 292.

[4] Vaz, *The Portuguese in California,* 91.

[5] M. da Silveira Cardozo, *The Portuguese in America 590 BC-1974,* (Dobbs Ferry, NY, 1976), 34.

[6] Ibid., 46-47.

[7] Vaz, *The Portuguese in California,* 80.

[8] D.R. Taft, *Two Portuguese Communities in New England,* (New York, 1923), 97.

[9] Vaz, *The Portuguese in California,* 19.

[10] A.R. Graves, "Immigrants in Agriculture: The Portuguese Californians, 1850-1970s," (Ph.D. dissertation, University of California, Los Angles, 1977), 11-12.

[11] Leo Pap, *Portuguese American Speech: An Outline of Speech Conditions Among Portuguese Immigrants in New England and Elsewhere in the United States,* (New York, 1949), 13.

[12] Graves, "Immigrants in Agriculture: The Portuguese Californians, 1850-1970s," 10-11.

[13] G.A. Estep, "Portuguese Assimilation in Hawaii and California," *Sociology and Social Research* 26: 64.

[14] Diane Amaral Lane, "Portuguese Religious Festivals," (MA Thesis, California State University, Chico, 1978), 22-23.

[15] Estep,"Portuguese Assimilation in Hawaii and California," 68.

[16] Lane, "Portuguese Religious Festivals," 65-77.

[17] Ibid., 74-77.

[18] Estep, "Portuguese Assimilation in Hawaii and California," 65.

[19] Francisco Cota Fagundes, "O Falar Luso-Americano: Um Indice de Acculturação," *First Symposium on Portuguese Presence in California,* (San Franciso, 1974), 17. My translation of the quote.

[20] Ibid., 8-17.

[21] Geoffrey L. Gomes, "Bilingualism Among Second and Third-Generation Portuguese-Americans in California," *First Symposium on Portuguese Presence in California,* (San Francisco, 1974), 45

[22] Estep, "Portuguese Assimilation in Hawaii and California," 63.

[23] Hans Howard Leder, "Cultural Persistence in a Portuguese-American Community," (Ph.D. dissertation, Stanford University, 1968), 88-89.

177

Why did the Azoreans not migrate to Continental Portugal ?

BOOKS

Açores: Do 25 de Abril até aos nossos dias. 1977. Lisboa.

Anderson, Grace M., and D. Higgs. 1976. *A Future to Inherit: The Portuguese Communities of Canada*. Toronto: McClelland and Stewart.

Anderson, Grace M. 1974. *Networks of Contact: The Portuguese and Toronto*. Ontario: Wlifrid Laurier University.

Berger, Josef. 1941. *In Great Waters: The Story of the Portuguese Fishermen*. New York: The Macmillan Group.

Boissevain, Jeremy. 1974. *Friends of Friends: Networks, Manipulators and Coalitions*. Oxford: St. Martin's Press.

Brettell, Caroline B. 1977. Ethnicity and Entrepreneurs: Portuguese Immigrants in a Canadian City. In *Ethnic Encounters: Identities and Contexts*, ed. George L. Hicks and Philip E. Leis, 170-80. North Scituate, MA: Duxbury Press.

Brown, Walton John. 1972. *A Historical Study of the Portuguese in California*. San Francisco: R&E Research Associates.

Cardozo, Manoel da Silveira. 1976. *The Portuguese in America 590 B.C.-1974*. Dobbs Ferry, NY: Oceana Publications.

Crissey, F. 1914. *Where Opportunity Knocks Twice*. Chicago.

Dana, Richard Henry. 1936. *Two Years Before the Mast, A Personal Narrative of Life at Sea*. NewYork: Harper & Brothers.

DeVos, George, and Lola Romanucci-Ross, ed. 1975. *Ethnic Identity: Cultural Continuities and Change*. Palo Alto: Mayfield Publishing Company.

Felix, John Henry, and Peter F. Senecal. 1978. *The Portuguese in Hawaii*. Honolulu: The Authors.

Goode, George Brown. 1887. *The Fisheries and Fishery Industries of the United States*, 5 Vols. Washington, DC: Government Printing Office.

Guill, James H. 1972. *A History of the Azores Islands*. Menlo Park, CA.

Halley, W. 1876. *The Centennial Year Book of Alameda County, California*. Oakland, CA.

Henriques, Borges de. 1867. *A Trip to the Azores or Western Islands*. Boston: Lee and Shepard.

Housby, T. 1971. *The Hand of God: Whaling in the Azores*. New York: Abelard-Schuman.

Jenkins, James Travis. 1971 [1921]. *A History of the Whale Fisheries*. New York.

Kuykendall, Ralph Simpson. 1967. *The Hawaiian Kingdom, Vol III, 1874-1893. The Kalakaua Dynasty*. Honolulu: University of Hawaii.

Leading Manufacturers and Merchants of Eastern Massachusetts: 188? Historical and Descriptive Review of the Industrial Enterprises of Bristol, Plymouth, Norfolk and Middlesex Counties. New York.

London, J. 1914. *The Valley of the Moon.* New York.

Melville, Herman. 1950 [1851]. *Moby Dick or The Whale.* New York: Gilberton.

Morison, Samuel Eliot. 1921. *The Maritime History of Massachusetts 1783-1860.* Boston: Houghton Mifflin Company.

Namais, June. 1978. *First Generation: In the Words of Twentieth-Century American Immigrants.* Boston: Beacon Press.

Nordhoff, Charles. 1874. *Northern California, Oregon, and the Sandwich Islands.* New York: Harper & Brothers.

Oliver, L. 1972. *Never Backward: The Autobiography of Lawrence Oliver—A Portuguese-American.* San Diego: Neyenesch.

Orbach, M.K. 1977. *Hunters, Seamen, and Entrepreneurs: The Tuna Seinermen of San Diego.* Berkeley.

Pap, Leo. 1949. *Portuguese-American Speech: An Outline of Speech Conditions Among Portuguese Immigrants in New England and Elsewhere in the United States.* New York: King's Crown Press.

_____. 1976. *The Portuguese in the United States: A Bibliography.* New York: Center for Migration Studies.

Pease, Zeph.W., and George A. Hough. 1889. *New Bedford, Massachusetts: Its History, Institutions and Attractions.* New Bedford: Mercury Publishing Company.

Scammon, Charles Melville. 1874. *The Marine Mammals of the North-Western Coast of North America.* San Francisco: J.H. Carmany and Company.

Starbuck, Alexander. 1964. *History of the American Whale Fishery From Its Earliest Inception to the Year 1876,* 2 vols. New York: Argosy-Antiquarian.

Taft, Donald R. 1923. *Two Portuguese Communities in New England.* New York: Columbia University.

Taylor, Phillip. 1971. *The Distant Magnet: European Emigration to the U.S.A.* New York: Harper & Row.

Trueblood, M.A. 1977. The Melting Pot and Ethnic Revitalization. In *Ethnic Encounters: Identities and Contexts,* ed. George L. Hicks and Philip E. Leis, 153-67. North Scituate, MA: Duxbury Press.

Vaz, A.M. 1965. *The Portuguese in California.* Oakland, CA: I.D.E.S. Supreme Council.

Walker, Walter Frederick. 1886. *The Azores or Western Islands: A Political, Commercial and Geographical Account.* London: Trubner & Co.

Wolfbein, S.L. 1944. *The Decline of a Cotton Textile City: A Study of New Bedford.* New York: Columbia University Press.

Wolforth, Sandra. 1978. *The Portuguese in America.* San Franciso: R & E Researh Associates.

Young, M.F., comp. 1973. *The Portuguese in Hawaii: A Resource Guide.* Honolulu.

PERIODICALS

Bruemmer, F. Survival of American Whaling Terms in the Azores. *American Speech* 35 (1): 20-23.

Clarke, R. 1954. 'Open Boat Whaling in the Azores' (The History and Present Methods of a Relic Industry). *Discovery Reports* 26: 281-354.

Davis, K. 1974. The Migrations of Human Populations. *Scientific American* 231 (3): 92-105.

d'Oliveira Baptista, João, and Vincente d'Ornellas. 1970. Destination, Sandwich Islands, Nov. 8, 1887. [Trans. L. de Silva Canario.] *The Hawaiian Journal of History* 4: 3-52.

Estep, G.A. 1941. Portuguese Assimilation in Hawaii and California. *Sociology and Social Research* 26: 61-69.

Fagundes, Francisco Cota. 1974. O Falar Luso Americano: Um Indice de Aculturação. *First Symposium on Portuguese Presence in California* [UPEC Cultural Center and the Luso-American Education Foundation]: 8-17.

Gomes, G.L. 1974. Bilingualism Among Second and Third Generation Portuguese-Americans in California. *First Symposium on Portuguese Presence in California* [UPEC Cultural Center and the Luso-American Education Foundation]: 45-46.

Meisler, S. 1978. Portuguese in Canada Cling to Old Ways. *Los Angeles Times,* December 5.

Rogers, F.M. 1974. Americans of Portuguese Descent: A Lesson in Differentiation. *Sage Research Paper in the Social Sciences.*

Silva, P.T., Jr. 1976. The Position of 'New' Immigrants in the Fall River Textile Industry. *International Migration Review* 10 (2): 221-232.

Sklarewitz, N. 1979. Portugal: Slow Going Toward Strong Democracy. *The Christian Science Monitor,* March 20.

Williams, F. G. 1974. Os Inícios da Pesca do Atum em San Diego. *First Symposium on Portuguese Presence in California* [UPEC Cultural Center and the Luso-American Education Foundation]: 6-7.

GOVERNMENT PUBLICATIONS

Canada, Census of Population, 1996.

Census of the Population, 1990. United States Summary; Population for Selected Ancestry Groups.

Census of the Population, 1960. 1960 Vol.1, *Characteristics of the Population;* Part l, *United States Summary;* Part 6, *California;* Part 8, *Connecticut;* Part 13, *Hawaii,* Part 23, *Massachusetts,* and Part 41, *Rhode Island.* Washington, DC.

Eighth Census of the United States, 1860. 1864 Vol. 1, *Population of the United States in 1860.* Washington, DC.

Fifteenth Census of the United States, 1930. 1930 Outlying Territories and Possessions; and *Vol. 3, Population,* Part 1. Washington, DC.

Fourteenth Census of the United States, 1920. 1920 Vol. 3, *Population,* Washington, DC. 1920

Godsil, H.C. 1938 *The High Seas Tuna Fishery of California.* Fish Bulletin No. 51, Bureau of Marine Fisheries, Division of Fish and Game of California. Sacramento.

Immigration and Naturalization Service, 1976 Annual Report. 1977 (various years from l959-1976). United States Department of Justice, Washington, DC.

Immigration Statistics Canada, 1970. 1970 (various years from 1971-1977). Department of Manpower and Immigration, Ottawa.

Ninth Census of the United States, 1870. 1872 Vol. 1. Washington, DC.

População dos Açores. 1975. Departmento Regional e Estudos e Planeamento, Açores.

IX Recenseamento Geral da População no Continente e Ilhas Adjacentes em 15 de Dezembro 1950 de 1952. 1952 Tomo II. Instituto Nacional de Estatística, Lisboa.

X Recenseamento Geral da População no Continente e Ilhas Adjacentes, 1960. 1960 Tomo II. Instituto Nacional de Estatística, Lisboa.

XI Recenseamento da População Continente e Ilhas Adjacentes de 1970. 1970 Instituto Nacional de Estatística, Lisboa.

XIV Recenseamento Geral da População, Açores, 2001.

Starks, E.C. 1922. *A History of California Shore Whaling.* Fish Bulletin No. 6, State of California Fish and Game Commission, Sacramento.

Súmula de Dados Estatísticos. 1976. Departamento Regional de Estudos e Planeamento, Açores.

Thirteenth Census of the United States, 1910. 1910 Vol. II, *Population.* Washington, DC.

Twelfth Census of the United States, 1900. 1900 Vol. II, *Population,* Part II. Washington, DC.

U.S. Congress, Senate Report of the U.S. Immigration Commission, 1911 Vol. 24, Pt. II, *Immigrant Farmers in the Western States,* Chap. XIV. "Portuguese Farmers About San Leandro, California," Pp. 489-493. Washington, DC.

UNPUBLISHED MATERIAL

Alves, A. 1978. Interviewed in Patterson, CA, on Nov. 25.

Avila, J. 1978. Interviewed in Modesto, CA, on Nov. 24.

Chang, M. 2002. Unpublished family history.

Diniz, M. 1978. Interviewed in Patterson, CA, on Nov. 25.

Estep, G.A. 1941. Social Placement of the Portuguese in Hawaii as Indicated by Factors in Assimilation. M.A. thesis, University of Southern California.

Ferst, S.T. 1972. The Immigration and the Settlement of the Portuguese in Providence: 1890 to 1924. M.A. thesis, Brown University.

Fielding, G.J. 1961. Dairying in the Los Angeles Milkshed: Factors Affecting Character and Location. Ph.D. dissertation, University of California, Los Angeles.

Graves, A.R. 1977. Immigrants in Agriculture: The Portuguese Californians, 1850-1970s. Ph.D. dissertation, University of California, Los Angeles.

Immigration and Naturalization Service, Washington, DC. Information on the number and location of permanent resident Portuguese aliens in the United States for 1977 and 1978.

Lane, D.A. 1978. Portuguese Religious Festivals. M.A. thesis, California State University, Chico.

Leder, H.H. 1968. Cultural Persistence in a Portuguese-American Community. Ph.D. dissertation, Stanford University.

Loosley, A.C. 1927. Foreign Born Population of California in 1848-1920. M.A. thesis, University of California, Berkeley.

Maciel, E. 1978. Interviewed in Modesto, California, on Nov. 24.

Smith, M.E. "Estão aqui Mesmo." Paper written by Smith, as an Anthropologist at SUNY-Brockport.